Why Epiphanies Never Occur to Couch Potatoes

Mark Amtower

Advance Comments for
Why Epiphanies Never Occur to Couch Potatoes

"Though this book will only take you a short time to read, the lessons you learn will last a lifetime."

Rieva Lesonsky
Editorial Director, Entrepreneur *magazine*

"'The Speech' was one of the finest I have ever heard—from the heart and constructed of timeless integrity and wisdom. Now, the book tells us what lies behind the speech and it makes it all the more important to read and hear this brilliant, multi-faceted jewel, this treasure of honest writing."

Don Libey
Libey Incorporated

"There are very few people who can write and speak with equal ease on highly specialized topics as well as broad big-picture notions. Mark Amtower is one of them. He is best-known as America's leading expert on marketing to government. In *Why Epiphanies Never Occur to Couch Potatoes*, he widens his focus to dispense wisdom won from the school of hard knocks—common-sense advice and practical ideas that can help you achieve greater success in every important area of your life."

Robert (Bob) W. Bly
World-renowned copywriter, author of over 70 books

"Finally a book I can recommend to family and friends. An enjoyable set of stories containing profound life lessons I wished I'd learned 20 years earlier!"

Bill Harrison
FreePublicity.com

"Fun, easy and real. Amtower's outlook on life is simple and unpretentious. I kept finding myself thinking of my own life priorities."

Bob Prosen
Best-selling author of Kiss Theory Goodbye

"What a little gem of a personal statement. Don't let the wry title mislead you: Mark Amtower holds back nothing, neither in his personal history nor in his personal philosophy. Statements such as 'Fidelity is its own reward' and the more abstruse but certainly profound 'The Law of Divine Right to Attention' are worthy of consideration even by those who regard themselves as super sophisticates."

Herschell Gordon Lewis
Direct marketing author and columnist

"Some people make great works of art. Some people build giant corporations.

Some people attain high office and bend others to their will. And some people merely go through the world, doing well by doing good. These are the ones who sleep best at night. Mark Amtower is such a person.

I've known Mark since we started our publishing company Key Communications Group in 1976. Mark was my list broker, helping me choose and obtain mailing lists that led to my company's early success.

Then Mark became an expert on mailing into the Federal government, just as we got into Federal HR. Once again, Mark gave us a leg up, and this time only Mark could do so. Mark was the only person alive who knew anything about this devilishly difficult task—and Mark seemed to know everything about it.

Mark entered the seminar business and invited me to speak at one of his "do's." That engagement led to a connection with National Audio-Visual Supply and its principal, Scott Heller, that has been one of the most rewarding business friendships I've enjoyed.

Then Mark introduced our publication, the *Federal Personnel Guide,* to his federal-marketplace clientele, with the happy result that four Amtower clients bought tens of thousands of copies of the *Guide.*

Did I make some money along the way? Most certainly. Did Mark? I hope so. As I said above . . . doing well by doing good has been Mark's way for the thirty-plus years I've known him.

How would you like to succeed the Mark Amtower way? You can . . . because now Mark has written it all down in *Why Epiphanies Never Occur to Couch Potatoes.*

I'd call this a how-to book but it's really more of a why-I-did book. Mark spells out the beliefs that have inspired his professional life. Beliefs like

- Why relationships matter more than dollars (and why good relationships often result in dollars).
- "Tithing" as a secret of success.
- The bottom-line benefits of being loyal.
- The law of market ownership, and how to respect it.

Mark portrays himself herein as "not God's brightest child." If this book has a flaw, I'd say it was false modesty. Mark is among God's brighter children, I am here to tell you, and anyway—as Mark himself immodestly says—he is among God's most persistent children.

There's much more here, delivered in Mark's own folksy style—a philosophy of life translated into business success terms, with entertaining asides and charming cartoon illustrations to make the medicine go down.

Will Mark's aphorisms work for you? That is for you to find out, and I encourage you to do so. That they worked for Mark is beyond question."

Frank Joseph
Long-time Amtower friend and author of To Love Mercy

"Mark Amtower proves you can achieve greater success in business and in life than you ever imagined possible. He shows you how to stop letting perfectionism and other excuses from holding you back and start creating your dreams."

Steve Harrison
Co-founder, FreePublicity.com

To Mary Ellen,
Elora, and Travis,
whose opinions of me matter most.

"Keep away from people who try to belittle your ambitions. Small people always do that, but the really great make you feel that you, too, can become great."

Mark Twain

"The voice of one crying out in the wilderness . . ."

Matthew, 3:3

"Nel mezzo del camin di nostra vita."
("How do I see my life, moving steadily upwards?")

Dante, Divine Comedy

Acknowledgments

Cartoonist and caricaturist Dave McCoy was referred to me by my friend Bob Bly (yes, Robert W. Bly), who uses his cartoons frequently in his own work. I thought I had a caricaturist, but he seemed to disappear, so I went looking, and here are the results. This is not to say Dave is a second choice—I love the results. I hope you enjoy them as much as we did at my house.

My friends Shelley Sapyta, Elaine Lattanzi, and others at BookMasters handled the cover design and book layout, and as always, surpassed my expectations.

Don Libey suggested the book immediately after the speech that started it all. Don also did the first edit.

My friend Bob Davis coined the phrase about market ownership, "Marketshare is rented—never owned," in Law 4. Thanks for letting me use it, Bob.

My wife, Mary Ellen, and her parents (who live with us), Matt and Georgiana Podniesinski, are always among my early editors. Mary Ellen read the manuscript several times for me—for which I am extremely grateful. And my children, Elora and Travis, who put up with my work habits.

And throughout the book you will see others I acknowledge. This is the tip of the iceberg. There are hundreds who have provided much along the way, but as I say several times, this is a short book. Perhaps we can address a few of them in the next book. . . .

Contents

Foreword

David Powell, Federal Business Council, Inc.

About seven years ago I got a phone call that lasted about 30 seconds. Imagine a gruff, deep voice in the cadence of a drill instructor, "This is Amtower, we need to meet." That was it.

Those of you who know Mark will understand but at the time I thought "who does this guy think he is?" We ended up meeting for lunch and it was the beginning of not only a business relationship but a great friendship that continues to surprise me, educate me, and push me in new directions.

Mark invited me to hear him speak at the MeritDirect conference in 2005. First let me give you some background. Mark is always spot-on in his assessment of the marketplace. He works with some of the most successful people in the market. He's a rare commodity. He gets results. He's opinionated. He's direct. What he isn't is diplomatic. He tells it like it is and usually in the most colorful language possible. (Personally, I find this refreshing.)

Back to the conference—I did not know what Mark was going to speak about, but based upon personal experience I thought he wanted me to give him a signal if he was being "too colorful." However, he went into this new presentation of his thoughts on success in life, which we've later come to know as his "epiphanies."

So while I sat through the Epiphanies speech I experienced a dynamic in the audience that I had not seen before. Everyone was listening. Everyone was paying extremely close attention. I am in the conference business and see hundreds of presentations every year but this one seemed to resonate across the board. Mark connected on that day with everyone in the room, including me.

I took notes of everything he said and when I got back to my hotel room I used it to examine my own life in each one of the categories and have worked on it every day since. I'm fairly sure many other audience members did the same thing. I told Mark after his speech that I thought this would make a great book and if he was looking for the material for the next one, he had it in his hands. I'm glad to see he's done it.

Sometimes it's the message and other times the messenger that makes something meaningful. In this case it's both the message and the messenger combined that make this such a compelling look at how to be successful in life.

David Powell, Vice President and
COO, Federal Business Council
Friday, May 4, 2007

Author's Preface

Epiphany (noun); 1. a. A Christian feast celebrating the manifestation of the divine nature of Jesus to the Gentiles as represented by the Magi. b. January 6, on which this feast is traditionally observed. 2. A revelatory manifestation of a divine being. 3. a. A sudden manifestation of the essence or meaning of something. b. A comprehension or perception of reality by means of a sudden intuitive realization. *(For the purposes of this book, we are dealing with the third definition, parts a and b.)*

This book started as a luncheon speech at the Merit Direct B-to-B Co-op on July 14, 2005. The speech and now this book have been a companion ever since, reminding me that there is much more to communicating besides words. And speaking of communicating . . .

My speaking coach, **Maggie Bedrosian**, wrote this about our first encounter: "I think we first met at the Tower Club in Virginia. I was amazed at his earthy, opinionated style. 'How does he survive,' I asked myself, 'in the business environment where a polished patina often outshines real content?'"

Many people feel this way after a "close encounter" with the anomaly I seem to be. You may feel that way while you are reading this book.

This is my book. By that I simply mean these are my thoughts on how I should live my life. It started as a lunch speech at a marketing conference and has taken on a life of its own. Written to give people a different and closer look at who I am, after it was written and the speech delivered, it simply would not leave me alone.

I have high expectations of myself beyond goals: behavioral standards. The attainment of the goals is great, but how I get there is more important. It was not until I started enumerating my rules of conduct, committing them to paper and then further scrutiny, that I started to be more consistent in my actions and more reliable to myself.

I have a hard enough time staying within the boundaries I set for myself, so I neither seek nor hope for blind acceptance or agreement with what I write and I do not expect many—if any—people to agree with me on all things presented herein. I hope you have your own rules of conduct, and I hope you write them down.

Without these, how do we teach our children? It is not the rules that will teach, but the more consistent actions that result from written rules that will teach.

I *do* hope for those who read this to look more carefully at shiny rocks, watch out for *cider in the ear* and other forms of subterfuge, deception, and trickery that I will address as you proceed.

I am also aware these are *not* new ideas. What is new here is my perspective, my way of relating these to my life, and my selection of what is most important and why it was selected.

◊   ◊   ◊

Headlines abound with excesses and misdeeds from the world of business, politics, the fourth estate, academia, religion, science—everywhere. People taking money on the sly, hoping against hope not to get "caught in the act"; politicians, parish priests, and ministers abusing their positions for personal gain or baser desires; writers claiming the works of others as their own; web sites offering students pre-fabricated reports and papers; scientists falsifying lab results; executives falsifying financial reports. Everywhere there seems to be deception for reasons that seem stupid when they get caught, if they get caught. Apparently during the act there is some form of denial that "ever so bright me will never be caught."

Television, radio—indeed, *all media exacerbate* this with provocative teasers: "next on (put the name of any show here). . . ." One minute they are making people stars and celebrities and the next they are lamenting the excesses with all the sincerity Claude Rains shows in *Casablanca* when he closes Rick's because he "is shocked to find gambling," as he receives his winnings on the side.

This is all followed by verbal moral outrage, then more of the same. The cycle continues unabated: adoration, revelation, outrage, hand-wringing, the adoration for something new but oh-so similar.

Many personal actions are condoned and rationalized as *situational* until someone demonstrates that the emperor indeed has no clothes.

Situational ethics is a crutch for the ethically impaired. There is right and there is wrong. There is that which you can explain to your children and that which you cannot. The "lesser of two evils" does not imply a good.

Finally, this is my quest for the ultimate attitudinal differentiator. To me, my attitude is everything, but it is attitude built on the belief that I am who I think I am. My confidence in what I say and do seems to set me apart. In my experience, the happier I am with who I am becoming (I am far from done with my evolution), the more I do to further that progress. The result for me is my extremely positive attitude.

My speaking coach, Maggie Bedrosian, once told me I talked too much about others during my business presentations and not enough about myself. Part of what I am known for is my ability to share both the credit and the spotlight, and I do not feel this has diminished me in any way. I know it adds, and makes others want to be part of that circle I am sharing. These are small good deeds.

I experience joy with each small good deed I do, regardless of whether or not the deed has a witness. This type of inclusiveness offers me another form of communion. *God lets no deed, good or bad, go unnoticed.*

Warning to the Reader

I am not necessarily a linear writer or thinker. This has been apparent to many who have attended my events over the years, but most don't seem to mind. It was apparent to my teachers when I was in school, and they did mind.

Things occur to me in a sequence of their own choosing, and though I occasionally attempt to put these thoughts in some sort of logical sequence, I am often thwarted in the attempt by some other tangential thought that . . . where was I?

Why This Book?

Like Steinbeck, I set this down not so much to inform others but to remind myself. This book started as a lunch speech at the 2005 Merit Direct Business Co-op, and it is a short book. What do you want—the speech was only 20 minutes!

Like me and many of the other presenters at this event, most of the attendees are regulars. Most of these people know who I am, know what my specialty is (I am a nationally recognized expert in marketing to the government), and have a feel for *who* I am.

So I decided to do something different at lunch. A couple of years before at this same event, I did what has become my *Ten Myths of the Government Market* speech, a lighthearted look at why many companies don't do well in the government market. I wanted something in the same vein, a Letterman kind of countdown, but I did **not** want to talk about the government market. Not everyone who attends is interested in the government market.

I wanted to strike a more personal note, to connect at a different level.

So I started making some notes on a talk that was to become *Amtower on Survival and Success*—my laws, learned in the trenches—the rules that I choose to live by.

I was a little nervous when I got up to speak at that lunch, not knowing what these people who thought they knew me would think of this . . . *sermon.* I had to work from my notes as I had not memorized the speech.

Although it was only 20 minutes long, I was still tweaking it 30 minutes before lunch. I do that way too often!

A minute or so after I started talking I hit my comfort zone, and feeling comfortable, I referenced several people in the room when it was germane to the talk. I had lots of friends in that room, people I had worked with for years. And there were several of my personal advisors in that room—among them **Ralph Drybrough, Don Libey,** and

David Powell, but this time they had no idea what I was going to talk about.

During the speech I made eye contact with as many people as I could, while still knowing where I was in the script of the speech. It seemed very quiet, my tone increasing in confidence with every sentence. I was feeling very good about this talk.

And suddenly it was over and there was applause. The speech was only 20 minutes, and the 200 or so attendees seemed to like it. Or maybe they liked that it was short.

The event photographer, **Mike Pierro** of Vita Photo, came up to me and said it was the only lunch event he had ever shot where every eye was on the speaker and there were *absolutely no side conversations,* not even in whispers. I was flattered and stunned.

Several people, maybe as many as one-third of those in attendance, came up to thank me over the next several hours for the speech, and many of these asked for a transcript, starting with **Irv Greenberg** of ATD. Irv knows me well, having been a client for several years.

Then Don Libey said, "This is a whole new level, Mark. This is your next book." Then David Powell said the same thing.

The seed was planted. And now the book is **written, *but never quite done.***

Why Me?

Why *not* me?

In my market, I often say things that other people are thinking, but have neither the venue nor desire to say out loud. As the way I say things can often be edgy, many people read my e-newsletter and listen to my radio show. My candor has created a significant audience.

My edge has always been there, as it makes things more fun for me. It is part of that attitude. But the edge is not designed to be mean-spirited, just factual. I try not to launch personal attacks, and when I am on or near the edge, there are a couple people in my market I ask for advice. **Olga Grkavac** and **Anne Armstrong** have been kind enough to work with me on many occasions to keep me from going over that edge.

I think many people have books in them that just never come out. I think many people have great ideas that, for many reasons, never come to fruition. I have no desire to be a person who says things like, "I could have done that," or "I had that same idea years ago." *These are the swan songs of the couch potato,* the person who always has something impeding the thought-meets-action process. The impediment often takes the form of a sporting event, a "reality" show, the sports page, or something else on television, providing a seemingly acceptable rationale for inaction, or as it is often viewed, delayed action. It is simply delayed *ad infinitum.*

Well meaning as they may be, as a rule, *these are not the people likely to cause an epidemic of goal-direct actions in their immediate vicinity.*

I have no desire to join their ranks. I am almost always carrying a pen and pad in case of an outbreak of the ever-elusive great line or other random thought that occurs at strange times. I will get up in the middle of the night to write down one sentence, or an entire line of thought. My children often ask why I make notes during Mass. I will call my office answering machine if I am driving to record thoughts. *I am loathe to let thoughts escape unnoticed, unexamined, and unused.*

So, why me? First, I have read several books in ethics/morality/success space and several of them are quite good.

Several others are the reading equivalent of watching paint dry. Only a few writers and speakers, Jim Rohn, Zig Ziglar, Mark Victor Hansen, Chris Gardner, Lee Milteer, and Charlie "Tremendous" Jones, in particular, move me to action. If you want or need to read a truly inspiring story, read "The Pursuit of Happyness."

Further, I believe I bring a different perspective, having started with a business speech on Survival and Success and evolving into a practical philosophy for living, while retaining the edge that sets me apart. The message, as a result, might get through to broader audiences.

As I mentioned in the Warning to the Reader, I am not linear in my approach, so I needed something—somewhere—to start a continuing dialogue with myself, then include others. I needed to create a forum, somewhere I could place these random thoughts for further perusal and discussion. Writing the book was the dialogue with myself; people reading the book broadens the dialog; www.EpiphanyBook.com will allow readers to share thoughts with each other and me, continuing the dialog. So during your journey through this brief book, should you desire to share your thoughts, go to www.EpiphanyBook.com, register, and share on the blog.

CHAPTER 1

Something Concrete You Can Rely On

"We cannot live our lives on our own terms unless and until we know what those terms are."

Amtower-ism

I am not God's brightest child. I have never been a quick learner, often to the chagrin of parents and teachers. This has not bothered me since I was about twelve. It has been said that subtlety is wasted on me. While this may or may not be true, I have yet to lose sleep over it.

Nor am I among His quickest children. I like to observe and absorb, and often take longer than many to reach my conclusion, unless my mouth decides to voice a conclusion before my brain is finished. Most of the time I do not like to feel like I am rushed (though my children may feel differently when I am driving). I do not wear a watch, as I tend to operate at my own pace, and for most things during my normal day I do not need to know the time. This is can be a great perk when you work for yourself, if you are able to take advantage of it.

I am, however, among His most persistent. Many things do not come easy for me, but once I catch on, they

1

tend to stay with me. I can put something down for a while—often a long while—then come back, pick it up, and proceed.

One desire that has been recurrent in my life is a need for a **constant**—something concrete, perhaps evolving, but something I can count on, like the security blanket Linus uses in the "Peanuts" comic strip. Many people seem to share this need and it can take different forms: members of your family, a particular place you can go, certain friends, or religion or its earthly representative—a pastor, priest, or rabbi.

But each of these is outside of our direct influence, and under adverse or extreme circumstances, far beyond our control to provide what we may need. *We cannot expect others to live up to our expectations* regardless of how well-intentioned they might be, because their expectations will be different from our expectations. The family members can move away or die, the special place may belong to someone else or be torn down, the friends can move on, and the earthly representatives of our religion may—or may not—be as helpful as we need them to be at certain times.

So, slow steady Mark comes up with a new/old idea: What if, just perhaps, we can count more on ourselves, like the Self-Reliance as espoused by Ralph Waldo Emerson in 1841, and strive to be the most consistent thing in our own lives? *Net e quaesiveris extra*—"do not seek outside yourself."

Then the issue becomes how?

Are we strong enough to be constants for ourselves? We need to be able to believe that we will act, or react, in certain ways under certain circumstances if we are truly going to be able to count on ourselves. We all have hopes about how we will react in certain circumstances, but are we who we think we are when the situation arises?

Then the issue remains *how*? Well, that could pose a problem. And I may have a solution.

Most of us have heard of the studies from several years back about two groups of Harvard students, where one group wrote down their goals and the second group did not. These groups were tracked through their careers, and the group with written goals was financially more successful than those with no written goals. The written goals provided a *direction*. This is good to know, and goals are something we should all have.

But what does it have to do with the topic at hand? Well, let me offer a supposition. What if at the same time you were enumerating your goals you wrote down the ethical parameters you would operate within to attain those goals— the moral guideposts you would seek to use during your journey through life? If you had both the goals *and* the guidelines, could your life be more productive, satisfying, and meaningful? Or would the guidelines inhibit your ability to attain the goals? What good does this do in the "real world?"

Let me put this in a different way: Do you have any inviolable rule of conduct, a rule which you will not break, like your own Golden Rule? If so, have you written it down? If you have not written it down, has it become flexible over time? If you don't write it down, it may inadvertently become malleable.

Welcome to *situational ethics*, where all things are malleable, gray is the color of choice, and right and wrong become theoretical, not choices. In the world of situational ethics, excuses for actions or non-actions are plentiful, even something as seemingly mundane as holding the door for a senior citizen (I'm in a hurry . . .). Do not delude yourself—these are nothing but excuses.

So, what if someone comes along and offers you a *shiny rock*? Every day we are confronted by offers that seem to be shortcuts to success. We get assaulted by these from all media—television, the radio, in publications we read, phone calls we get, the people we see in the parking lot, the grocery store, or on an elevator. Too many people, it seems, are *looking for angles, not purposes*; a quick and easy ride to wealth, not the satisfaction of a life lived well. So when the shiny rock offer comes along, we are susceptible.

There is a scene in *Guys and Dolls* where Sky Masterson is offered a sucker bet by Nathan Detroit, who needs a quick ten grand. Sky does not fall for the bet, and reverses the tables. While doing so, he tells Nathan a story from his youth:

> *"On the day I left home to make my way in the world, my daddy took me to one side. 'Son,' my daddy says to me, 'I am sorry I am not able to bankroll you to a large start, but not having the necessary lettuce to get you rolling, instead, I'm going to stake you to some very valuable advice. One of these days, a guy is going to show you a brand-new deck of cards on which the seal is not yet broken. Then this guy is going to offer to bet you that he can make the jack of spades jump out of this brand-new deck of cards and squirt cider in your ear. But, son, you do not accept this bet because, as sure as you stand there, you're going to wind up with an ear full of cider.'"*

Most of us occasionally get cider in our ears because *we choose to believe* that not only are there shortcuts to wealth or happiness or sex or whatever, but that these shortcuts will find a way to reveal themselves almost exclusively to us (not everyone—just us!) and we best be ready to dive right in with little or no due diligence, even if the shortcut seems shady. Due diligence is not required because we know it is our time—right now! We have paid our dues (or so we think) and we'd best jump—like every other lemming. It's just like when you were a kid, saying, "But everybody else does it!" And your mother said something like, "If every kid stood in front of a moving train, would you join them?"

When you are ripe for it, someone or something will come along with the next great idea, you know the one, it's *almost but not quite too good to be true*, perhaps the "Dunkin Donut Diet" (I *knew* they were good for me!). When it presents itself to you, know it for what it is: *yet another alliterative delusion*. It will show up in your email, your mail box, at a business meeting, in a bar, at the gym—anywhere.

Most of us have fallen for more than a couple of these along Life's Boulevard. And we also knew (deep down) that it was too good to be true, but went ahead because we wanted it to be true, we were tired of waiting for our proverbial boat to come in. It is analogous to planning your retirement by buying lottery tickets; the payoff may be great, but the odds are a little long. Have you ever gone to a "free seminar" where, at the end, an offer is made "that is only good if you sign before you leave"? Laugh and leave. "Limited time" offers tend to be repeated, and you will have time for a little research.

I have always had some rules of personal conduct, but did not start writing them down until I started working for myself. I had known my last employer for some time, as our paths crossed during some of my previous employments. During my brief period of employment with this gentleman, it dawned on me that his business practices were not the sort I could condone.

So one afternoon, things came to a head and I took my Rolodex (yes, it was *that* long ago), stuck my head in his office, and indicated that I was leaving and not returning.

The subsequent story of the next 24 hours is vastly amusing but cannot be committed to paper. If you ever meet me ask about it.

I left this employment with no prospects for another job—and less desire to seek one. This was in mid-December 1984. The next day I did an assessment of myself: big mouth that operates with minimal supervision from brain, some skills in marketing, some contacts in my industry, and the idea that working for others would always entail living down to their expectations, not up to mine.

I will not delude myself or mislead you. I had no idea how to run a business, so naturally I started one. It took a while to actually make a living. My longtime friend and first accountant **Tom Barrett** can attest to the fact that I had no clue about running a business. But it happened.

One reason that I succeeded in business was that I cared about the quality of my work. Another reason, perhaps a much bigger one, was that the relationships I established mattered to me. This is not to say I developed relationships with everyone I met in business, but that when I met people I felt had similar values, I bothered to start a relationship. Even though we are talking 20+ years back, many of those relationships are going strong.

I did lots of favors, volunteered some time, and became part of a community. After a while, I gained some visibility in this community, and kept doing the same things. I became a recognized "expert" at one aspect of my market, and bothered to share much of what I learned. I also kept meeting more people from different parts of my market.

Because I bothered to care about what I do, and to share frequently and in many forums with those who wanted to know what I knew, more opportunities occurred. Some of these were *epiphanies presented as advice* from people who knew me and cared enough to point out some things to me. For whatever reason, these people bothered to care about me.

As I said, I am not God's brightest child, but occasionally things get through the first time. Here are a few examples (from many) of epiphanies from my business life.

In the late 1980s, my friend **Judy Bradt** was the Commercial Officer at the Canadian Embassy. She asked me to speak to a trade group that was attending a major industry event. Though I had spoken at association meetings and the like, this was my first real public presentation. I was scared out of my wits, and used lots of "ums" and "ers," made little eye contact, and thought I had blown it, until many people came up after to say thanks for the great information.

'I was flattered, but I knew I had to do more of this and I needed help if I was going to be any good at it. I got help in the form of speaking coach Maggie Bedrosian and got better—not great, but better. I still work hard at getting better in front of a crowd.

And Judy? Judy has had her own company for the past three years and I have had the pleasure of acting as mentor to help her miss many of my mistakes.

Not long after that speaking opportunity I held my first public seminar, the first of over one hundred.

Also not long after that (still late 1980s) I was talking to another friend of mine, **Joan April**. Up to this time I was selling data I compiled from various government sources. I always made sure the data was more accurate than anywhere else, but that was my business—quality, up to date, easy to use. Joan called occasionally, and this time when she was getting ready to hang up, she said, "What's great about talking to you is you never send me a bill." People might pay me for what I knew? What a concept!

The consulting side of my business was born, though it took me a while to figure out that consultants had to charge a fair amount of money to be taken seriously. Suffice it to say that I now charge a *"fair* amount" of money. And I still have occasion to talk to Joan.

So now Mark the consultant was off and running, or as some would come to see it, loose and dangerous. I was looking for people to irritate (and invoice) with my esoteric knowledge.

My expertise is marketing, so I thought I needed to talk to marketing people. Even though these people would come to my seminars or call me on occasion, they did not want me in their offices. It wasn't until I was lamenting this situation with my friend **Carol May**, telling her about one marketing manager who would not even take my calls. Carol was the marketing manager of one of the trade publications, *Federal Computer Week*, and she knew a lot of people. I knew her because we went to the University of Maryland at the same time and became friends. Carol laughed and said I shouldn't be talking to marketing managers, I should be talking to CEOs!

Within weeks I had an appointment with the CEO at that company. The company was Falcon Microsystems, and the CEO was **Dendy Young**. Dendy, the first of hundreds of CEOs to meet with me, is still a valued friend of mine. That first day, going to Dendy's office, the marketing guy looked at me with a very confused look.

During this period, I developed and maintained a friendship with a woman who wrote an occasional column for one of the trade publications, *Government Computer News—*

another place I worked briefly. The woman, **Lynn Bateman**, was an expert in the federal procurement regulations and consulted with many of the top companies in the market. Lynn was one of the two big consultants offering guidance on contracting and procurement at that time. I would occasionally call or visit her offices and she was kind enough to act as my unofficial mentor. Many times she would encourage, cajole, or otherwise offer direction. She taught me several things I took to heart: to trust my instincts, not to pull my punches when I was right, and to be known for honest views. Not all of these instructions were verbal. Lynn's competence and confidence came through with resounding clarity when she spoke publicly or privately. She knew her business and was confident in her ability.

I did my best to follow her footsteps and am happy to report she thinks I did pretty well—so far. Like Han Solo's advice to Luke after Luke shoots down one of the bad guys, I can hear Lynn telling me *"Don't get cocky, boy."*

I was busy trying to make my business a success and occasionally paying attention to some of these psychic road signs that God and my friends were putting up for me. Thankfully, when the signs were put up, at least some of them were pretty obvious. Remember, I am not God's quickest child.

After my first public seminars attracted people from outside of the Washington, D.C. area (*people came from other places to hear me?!?!?*—this concept is still flattering even after all these years), I got a call from one of the attendees—**Stan Yablonksi**, who is president of Data-Pages in New Jersey. Stan told me he had just returned from a pretty good business conference. Further, he said, this conference needed me to speak when it happened the next year.

The issue of course, was that the conference did not yet know it needed me. I contacted the people who ran the event: **Chuck Tannen**, who owned and managed the event, and **Ellen Shannon**, who worked closely with him. I told them who I was and what I did, and they did ask me to speak the next year, and several times after that. They were very gracious hosts for that event. Chuck would host a reception for all the speakers the evening before the event started, and when I showed up the first time, he took me around and introduced me to several of my fellow speakers, some of whom are good friends still. Among these are **JoAnna Brandi**, **Michael Brown**, **Tracy Emerick, Vic Hunter**, **Don Libey**, and **Mac McIntosh**. Some of these people have been on my personal Board of Advisors and others have served on my clients' Boards of Advisors, and all of them are not simply good at what they do, but they are great people to know. I was also able to expand my business into a whole new area.

That conference opened many doors, and without Stan, I would never have known about it. After my first presentation at *Direct Marketing to Business* the next year, one of the people in the audience asked me when my book was coming out. I said I did not have enough material for a book. An attendee, **Sheila Schaetzke** of National Business Furniture, proceeded to tell me my presentation had more useful material than most business books she had read. So the seed was planted—a book!

It took 11 years, but the book did come out. *Government Marketing Best Practices* was published in January 2005.

I started the book in the early 2000s, and made the mistake of telling my friend Dendy Young that I was working on it. In 2004, he finally asked when he could see it. Now I had to finish it. Dendy got kudos in the Acknowledgements, and Sheila is still a client and friend, 13 years later.

There have been many more epiphanies over the years, but in the early years of working for myself, these examples have always stood out, and these stories have stayed very close to me. To me they were very important events, dominoes if you will, created and pushed by people who mattered to me, and people who cared enough to share their thoughts with me.

I am equally certain that there have been many possible epiphanies that I missed.

While many may look at me as a "self-made man," it should be apparent by now that I am not. I have been molded and shaped by people who cared and by events that occurred as a result. The myth of the "self-made" person (man or woman) is largely that, a myth. We have all had a variety of catalysts and epiphanies that have shown the way. We, the "self-made" folks, have had a lot of work to do to capitalize on the opportunities, but we all had help. I like to think it takes a bigger person to acknowledge the help.

We all get help, directly and indirectly, and with perseverance, it pays. Remember, I am among His most *persistent* children.

CHAPTER 2

Epiphanies are Everywhere . . . and Nowhere

Every day, comprehension or perception of reality by means of sudden intuitive realizations, or epiphanies, occur to each of us. The difference is a few of us recognize at least some of them for what they are, nuggets in the streams of our lives. Often they will only mean something to you and no one else. This makes it no less valuable.

Consulting Secrets of *The Poky Little Puppy*

Several years back I was invited to speak at an event for people who decided they wanted to consult for a living. At that time I was on the Board of Advisors for the American Consultants League, one of the bodies that certified consultants. My friend **Bob Bly** (aka, Robert W Bly, world famous author and copywriter) recommended me. I was flattered to be asked to join the Board and to speak, and I was determined to write a presentation the likes of which they had never heard.

Differentiation is an important concept for consultants to grasp, and I was looking for a new way to teach the concept of how to differentiate yourself from others in your niche.

My children were still pretty young, and I enjoyed read-ing them stories at night. When I got the invitation to pres-ent at this consultants conference, I thought about children's books.

Books for children often carry multi-tiered lessons. Case in point, one of my favorites: *The Poky Little Puppy*. First published in 1942, it is the story of five little puppies that go for an unauthorized walk in the "wide, wide world—through the meadow . . . down the road, over the bridge, across the green grass, and up the hill, one after the other."

When they reach this destination, one of them is miss-ing. The other four look around, eventually spotting him "at the grassy place, near the bottom of the hill (where) he was running around, his nose to the ground." "What is he *doing*?" (my children and I say **DOOOIINNNNNNGGG**, each time making it longer than the last) the other four puppies wonder, and down they go to find out. The poky little puppy smells something—rice pudding! and off they go, home to their rice pudding.

The first lesson of *The Poky Little Puppy*? Use all of your senses to understand all the things are in your immediate vicinity. There may be hidden treasures.

There are three such adventures in the story, each one ending with the puppies getting scolded by their mother for venturing outside of their yard. In the first two adventures, the poky puppy gets home after the scolding (he's poky, right?) and eats the dessert his mother wouldn't let the oth-ers have, because they have been sent to bed without dinner (remember, this was written in the 1940s). After the final adventure, the other four puppies do a good deed and get to eat all the strawberry shortcake, leaving the poky puppy with nothing when he meanders home as the others are fin-ishing the dessert.

The final lesson: paying attention to detail is good only if you act quickly!

I had my plan. I told my daughter **Elora** (about eight years old at the time) that I was going to use *The Poky Little Puppy* in my speech. She scoffed and said no way.

Well, I did. I will admit I got very mixed results from the crowd, *but* I did have 200+ would-be consultants loudly saying *"DOOOIINNNNNGGG."* And I have a witness. My friend and advisor **JoAnna Brandi** was with me when I gave this presentation, providing moral support. It is always great to have a friendly face in the crowd when you are speaking to a whole new audience and giving a new talk. The event took place in Florida not far from where she lived so we were able to spend a few hours together and she was able to attend my talk. And, she can say *"DOOOOIIIINNNNNG!"* quite well.

CHAPTER 3

The Speech—MeritDirect, July 14, 2005

Renaissance Hotel, Westchester, NY

Amtower's Laws of Survival and Success
(This is the speech from which this book evolved, with minor edits)

One of the few times I worked for other people, I sold team building and corporate motivational training. The owner was rich, but greedy. He envied the speakers who were commanding $10,000 and up per day, and in the early 1980s, this was very good money. This guy wanted to mentor me in the art of becoming rich, but I was resistant. I was not resistant to the idea of becoming rich—I was resistant to the idea of him being my mentor, because he did not believe in or practice what he preached. Needless to say, I did not stay long.

I am not among the quickest of people, but I am among the most persistent. Over time, this makes up for many shortcomings. As a persistent person, some things have occurred to me over the years, things that seem to matter. These have evolved over time and have become my Laws, the rules of conduct I live by. I have set them down not so much to inform others but to remind myself.

I don't pretend to know much about "reality" television, or much about television in general. My viewing is largely limited to CNN, local news, the History channel, and occasionally poker or Country Music TV.

From what I hear, the TV show *Survivor* is predicated on a predator, screw-your-buddy philosophy. In real life this approach usually doesn't work. Are there exceptions—predators who prosper? Certainly, but they are exceptions. Further, their prosperity is defined exclusively in financial terms—much like my would-be mentor—not in all of the ways I measure prosperity. Finance—making money—is among my criteria, but it is far from alone and it is not on the top of my list. But when I follow my Laws, money seems to follow.

I bother to care about a number of things, among them

- I care what I think of myself, every morning and every night;
- I care what my wife and children think of me and my actions;

- I care about expanding my knowledge base;
- I care about finding venues to learn and share;
- I care about creating venues to learn and share;
- And I care about slowly, carefully expanding my circle of trusted friends and advisors with people of similar values. You are known by the company you keep, and I am proud of the friends and advisors I have in my life and in this room, Ralph Drybrough, Don Libey, and David Powell.

The maxim your mother taught you, "You are known by the company you keep," *also implies you keep company with yourself.* If you are not an honorable person, honorable and successful people will not wish to keep company with you.

I value trust and collaboration, building relationships that last through time and turbulence.

So sit back and relax—but don't relax too much. See if you agree with AND pass Amtower's Laws of Life-Survival and Success.

Law 10–The Law of Tithing

In order to be part of a *community*, business or social, you must contribute to the community. There are active and passive ways to contribute, on and off the radar ways you must contribute—but the higher you go, or want to go, in a community, the more visible and active the contribution must be. This does not mean all of your contributions must be public, but you have to be an active participant.

Participating in local and national organizations is a contribution—as long as you are active. Writing and speaking become a must if you want to migrate up the food chain, not a "maybe later."

Understand and practice this and you will have a strong basis for success.

Violate this—be only a taker—and you will never be a true insider, an accepted member of the community, and your growth will be severely limited.

You can never be a leader in any community without tithing.

Law 9–The Amtower Uncertainty Principle, or the Law of the Food Chain

The *Heisenberg Uncertainty Principle* states the more defined the location of an object, the less certain we are about the momentum.

The *Amtower Uncertainty Principle* states that most people do not accurately know or define their real market position, their position in the food chain. Some people publicly and privately overstate their position in the food chain and their respective momentum, thereby misleading potential friends, employees, employers, partners, prospects, customers—even their family.

This will inevitably lead to poor delivery on the promises and to the slowing of whatever momentum these people might have, thus deteriorating their market position.

Each of us has had the coworker who claims responsibility for anything that goes right, the hindsight prescience to humbly seek kudos for work performed by others. I have seen resumes that could indicate the Second Coming.

Most of us recognize hype for what it is, but there is always someone willing to buy the Brooklyn Bridge. Unfortunately for some, some of those in the gullible category are in positions of responsibility.

Knowing and accepting your current market position allows you to accurately plot a course for higher things.

Law 8–The Law of Communication

The Law of Communication is simple: be able to succinctly state who you are and what you do. Keep it simple and always be truthful. If the person or group you are talking to is interested in what you say, they will ask for more.

Poor communication leads to diminishing returns. Communicate well or die a slow death.

Good communication lays solid groundwork.

Great communication lays a great foundation for bigger things sooner.

Great communication also leaves an audience that will be more receptive the next time they see you.

I am a WYSIWYG, a one-song jukebox. My tune does not change from audience to audience. What I say in a boardroom with the executive team or the Board of Directors is the same thing I will say in the cafeteria with the marketing staff. I am too simple for subterfuge, and I like myself too much to lie.

And I have found that my opinions and my candor expand my audience, they do not shrink it.

Be straight and keep it simple.

Law 7–The Law of Fidelity

Fidelity is its own reward.

Loyalty to customers, vendors, partners, the press, employees, bosses, friends, investors—ANYONE who is capable of influence in your niche or your life, is critical to your survival and growth.

If you constantly switch vendors, employees, and/or partners, you will be viewed as unstable and untrustworthy. This is not something that escapes the community where you live and work.

Conversely, loyalty is also visible to the community at large. The Law of Fidelity allows those *outside* your current circle to see the value of being *inside* that circle.

How many people in your life have violated this principle?

And how many people in your life are there when you need them?

If you have too many of the former, and not enough in the latter, you are in the wrong environment for sustained growth.

Law 6–The Law of Divine Right to Attention

Each of us believes that we are important and that we add value. The outward reception of that premise is not a given until the outward perception of that aligns what we think and how the market views us.

Once these are in tandem—and until that alignment takes place, there is no guarantee that others will pay attention to anything we say, regardless of how or where we say it.

Even after alignment occurs, there is no guarantee of continued attention.

Some people evidently feel they have this divine right to your attention as they use extreme hyperbole in an attempt to position themselves as the sole savior and provider of your business and personal opportunities. If you listen to them (or read their emails or resumes), you might believe (and some actually do) that this person will cause the confluence of the absolute right elements at a time designated by no less an authority than Nostradamus and will produce results that will make Bill Gates, Michael Dell, and Sam Walton envious.

When you meet people driven by adjectival fervor, and if you accept their carefully crafted hyperbolic assertions, you would immediately know that if you are not associated with this particular person immediately, that life would not simply pass you by, but that it would come to a screeching halt. Time for the cyanide.

Like the Law of Communication, it is important to be truthful and simple to keep expectations realistic. Attention is earned. Like marketshare, its growth is incremental. *Fifteen minutes of fame does not occur for everyone,* and if it occurs for you be gracious in your acceptance of that time. This gracious behavior will ultimately lead to more attention from the right people.

Law 5—The Law of Spontaneous Generation

Following closely on the Law of the Divine Right to Attention is the Law of Spontaneous Generation. Neither mindshare nor marketshare occurs spontaneously with your first missive—the announcement of your arrival in an already crowded niche. No press release, direct mail letter, space ad, radio spot, or standing on a street corner shouting guarantees you anything. The universe is not required to stop, hold its breath, and await your announcement.

Regardless of the earth-shattering nature of your newly announced job, product, or service, mindshare and market-

share growth are incremental. They may gain momentum, but all growth is incremental—and none is guaranteed.

Shortly after 9/11, a rich guy who had made lots of money in publishing decided that the Federal market required his expertise in the form of a new publication. He allegedly identified 30,000 people who "needed" this information. So the *Federal Paper* was born. Prior to the launch they called me, seeking advice. I gave them free advice over the phone. Washington, D.C. does not need another news source. No one is starving for news there, and there is no niche unserved. They insisted they had market research. I knew the market research they had, as Washington is very indiscreet in sharing privileged information. So I said three sycophants with their boss in a closet with a six-pack is not research. For some reason, they hung up.

The *Federal Paper* folded after two issues. Rich people invariably think they know more (remember my would-be mentor), deserve more attention, and that their ideas will necessarily generate more money.

There is inevitability to this law: believing you are the exception to it will lead to rapidly shrinking prospects.

Law 4–The Law of Market Ownership

There is none. Marketshare is rented—never owned.

Like mindshare, it is easily replaced.

When some people or companies emerge as market leaders, this is often accompanied by a significant attitude change—hubris.

Often market leaders become bullies, which makes many wish and work for their demise.

No one stays on top forever.

Some think if they study the market leaders closely, they will find the magic formula. While you can learn valuable lessons studying market leaders, there are too many variables for a single formula to exist. Each situation has unique characteristics.

Anyone selling the concept of the magic elixir, the "success formula," is selling thin air.

The necessary constants are hard work and the application of observed current and emerging market conditions. Then more work.

Pay attention, don't get arrogant, and continue to learn. Now growth can happen.

Law 3–The Law of Creation

Epiphanies occur to the proactive. When an epiphany occurs to a couch potato, the reaction is usually to pop another soda and try to rid yourself of this bothersome idea.

An epiphany occurring to a couch potato is like a rare tropical flower in a valley where no person has ever gone: It may be a thing of beauty, but no one is there to enjoy it.

Bother to think about what you do, to develop and share opinions, and more ideas—more epiphanies—will occur. And action is likely to take place.

The Law of Creation demands that you create ideas and develop relationships where you can share these ideas. Ideas have value when they lead to action.

This leads to a radical concept: opportunity.

Opportunities will lead to the ability to do something—to create mindshare, the capacity to create excitement as only ideas can.

Mindshare becomes marketshare when action occurs.

Marketshare allows you to grow, and ultimately give back. And the more you give back, the more you receive. Of this I am living proof.

Understand the Law of Creation and you are Oh So Close to creating value and developing marketshare.

Law 2–The Law of Leverage

Archimedes said, "Give me a place to stand and the right lever, and I can move anything."

If you don't "own" your space—your niche, if you have violated any of the previous laws and have exaggerated your position in the universe or failed to properly explain what you offer, if in any way you do not have a legitimate claim to the space you call your own, *you can be moved.* Trout and Ries called this repositioning. And as Letterman would say, we all know how painful that can be.

However, if you have operated in accordance with the previous eight laws, you will occupy the high ground and those attempting to move you will find themselves on a teetering rock using a toothpick for a lever. Freud would say, a tool too small to accomplish the task. Or as Amtower might say, don't you hate it when ethical midgets bite your ankles.

Regardless of who you are and where you go, someone—some boss, coworker, or someone who reports to you—will seek to reposition you, almost always to their advantage. We have all been there before, and we will all be there again.

Don't overstate your position in the universe and you will only move of your own volition.

Law 1–The Law of Gravitational Pull

The Law of Gravitational Pull occurs when you have executed the other nine laws well. When your niche is mentioned, your name occurs. If you have executed exceptionally well, your name comes up quickly—maybe first.

Good and sometimes great things happen when you execute the above laws. Bad things can happen if you don't. The antithesis of the Law of Gravitational Pull is The Law of Marginalization. You can be marginalized *if*, when you are not present and your niche or name comes up, someone dismisses you with a wave of the hand. With the wave of a hand you become a peripheral player—at best a sideshow.

But if you have executed well, others will immediately jump to your defense, countering this slight.

If you define yourself in a readily discernable manner—in what you *say*, in what you *write*, and most importantly, in what you *do*—you will never leave yourself open to be defined and repositioned by others.

The last I heard about the man who wanted to be my mentor was that he was with wife number four, was fairly well-off, but remains envious of those who command more attention and money. He still does not accept that others have earned that attention.

The world we live in is a chaotic place, and we all need something *constant*. The more you can become that constant for yourself, the happier you will be.

I envy no one. I don't measure myself by what other people think of me. Hemingway said living well is the best revenge. Amtower says have no regrets, and few reasons for regrets, and you will do well.

Thank you.

CHAPTER 4

How These Epiphanies (Laws) Came to Be, and How They Apply in My Everyday Life

This was a lunch speech for a business conference, but as I was writing it, I knew it applied to all aspects of my life. These are things I have learned by observation, experience, reading, writing, praying—all manner of methods were employed in the accumulation of my laws.

As a lunch speech, I did not want it to come across as a sermon, but as a way of demonstrating you can have a great time while living an ethical life; indeed, a better time. It is important to me to be able to have a good time regardless of what I am doing.

It started early. As my father worked at least two jobs when I was young, and was not at home on a regular basis, I learned many rules of conduct from my mother. **Barbara Amtower**, nee Kingsnorth, was a war bride from England. She came from London, where she obtained a Bachelor's degree in International History from Kings College at Cambridge University, to Cumberland, Maryland, a fair-sized town filled with mostly small-minded people. This is not to belittle Cumberland, but like most small towns in America in post-WWII, outside of the war, there was not much traveling done, and consequently a limited view of the world.

Mom was a foreigner who had stolen the heart of a local boy.

I think the best way to tell you about my mother is to share the eulogy I wrote for her and read at her funeral service.

The Odyssey of Barbara Amtower: 1924–2004

Mom inspired me in many ways. In my eyes she lived a life filled with faith, hope, charity, and love.

Her father was a Methodist minister and her mother a teacher. She grew up in England during the depression. She was educated in boarding schools and at Kings College at Cambridge University, where she received a Bachelor's degree in International History.

She met my father in my grandfather's church in England during the war. My theory is Pop saw Mom and followed her to church, not realizing where he was going. They were married in that church, by her father, albeit somewhat later. My father returned to America with the GIs. Mom came over, pregnant and alone, on a ship.

Because of a mix up, my Uncle and Grandfather "missed the boat"—her boat, in New York. So she had to make her way to Cumberland, pregnant and alone.

London, England, to Cumberland, Maryland—not exactly the intellectual mecca of the Western Hemisphere. A war bride in a cultural backwater, not the most hospitable of environments. If that alone doesn't show an extraordinary degree of faith and hope, I don't know what does. I do not say this to belittle Cumberland. My brother and I were born there, but it is a small town, with all of the small-town attributes. It had all of my father's history, and none of Mom's.

We moved to Montgomery County in 1952-so she spent seven years in Cumberland, a stranger in a strange land. Montgomery County, while relatively undeveloped at the time, was light years away from Cumberland. Finally Mom was able to establish a life out of the shadow of the "Amtowers of Arch Street." And we found the recently established Hughes Methodist Church, which became a big part of her life, especially with friends like Eleanor Rieff and all the Circle ladies through the years.

Pop always worked at least two jobs, so Mom was my active role model while I was growing up. Many of my women friends say I am a good "hugger"—this I learned from my Mom. Early on she taught me, by example, that caring is not simply OK, but it is good, necessary.

Back then we had to go into D.C. to get to a department store. Even then, in the 1950s when money was scarce, she would give me pocket change when I asked so I could give it to people begging in the streets. We had a few street people even back then. It was OK to care, it was important to care.

In the 1960s, as a family, we were involved in the Poor People's Campaign, and helped build Resurrection City on the Mall in D.C. It was OK to care and hope. It was important.

When Paul and I got older, Mom finally took a job. She worked with disabled children in the county schools—children who needed help. This is where she met two of her best friends, Connie Sullivan and Mary Ann Busse. These are wonderful women who loved my mother—both my parents, and they remained dedicated, loving friends.

I never heard Mom bad-mouth anyone. She was never a mean-spirited person, and she was always patient—even with Paul and me, and between us we were capable of trying the patience of just about anyone, and we did it often.

Mom was extremely bright without ever being a show-off. She could do the Post crossword puzzle in about five minutes. She almost always scored 100 percent in the Word Power game in Reader's Digest. When Paul or I needed help in homework—outside of math—Mom was always available, and always knew something about the subject. She even answered most of the questions on Jeopardy—usually to herself, so as not to destroy any fragile egos in the immediate vicinity.

She taught me things I use actively in my business and in my daily life—one posted at my company web site and one published in my book on marketing. At my web site my first rule is that I do not do things I can't tell my mother (now my wife and children), so don't come to me with an ethically questionable deal. In my book, I write that business is no different than your personal life—the lesson all our mothers taught us, that you are known by the company you keep. This is a lesson that remains important everywhere, and throughout our lives.

I have one regret regarding my parents. My brother's children, Kellie and Chris, knew my parents well, loved them, and were loved by them.

By the time I had children, Pop was an invalid and Mom spent every waking hour taking care of him. My children never had a real chance to know and love my parents, and be loved by them.

These are some of the things that I remember about Mom:

- Saying prayers with her and Paul when we were children;
- Mom coming back from England with her accent, and me wondering why she talked so funny;
- Mom walking me to school on my first day of kindergarten, and me telling her she didn't have to pick me up—I was a big boy. We lived a block away from the school. Even I couldn't get lost;
- Her chocolate chip and snickerdoodle cookies—fresh out of the oven, they were to die for;
- Her laugh and her smile;
- The one time I ever heard her belch—and it was a small one, at a holiday meal. Paul and I were stunned—we had never heard such a sound from this wondrous and wonderful lady;
- I will remember letting her know, when I was a child, and more recently as she succumbed to her dementia, that she was loved. So many people here let her know during that dark time that she was loved, and I thank you and God for that;
- That it is not simply OK to care, but important to do so in many ways;
- And I'll remember that she loved me.

My mother was an extraordinary woman, who may have seemed ordinary to many. I hope that all mothers are extraordinary for their children.

In the final analysis, God gives us the capacity for many things, but these three remain: faith, hope, and love. And the greatest of these is love. That chapter in Corinthians describes my Mom. That God loves my mother is not something I simply believe, it is something I know.

These are things my Mother taught me. They are the legacy I hope to pass to my children.

Thanks for coming to America, Mom. I love you.

This is not to diminish the role my father, **Arthur Amtower**, played. I loved my father, but there were times when we were not close, probably because we were so much alike.

One lesson learned from Pop was a *work ethic.* Pop was a math teacher by day, tutor in the afternoon, and assistant pharmacist in the evening. He was always working a second or third job to make ends meet. Teachers were not paid much in the 1950s, 1960s, and 1970s, and as most of us recall, few teachers were really memorable.

Another lesson I learned from my father, perhaps one of the most important in my life, was to be very good at what I chose to do, and not be afraid of being different. During our entire lives, my brother **Paul** and I would run into people who had Pop as a teacher: a teller at the bank, a clerk in the grocery store, somebody you were working with. They were everywhere, and when they saw or heard our last name, the inevitable question came up: "Did your father teach math at Sligo?" While we were growing up, this was not necessarily good, as Pop was a demanding teacher.

He was also very innovative in his methods. If you showed up without a pencil (required in his room) he would rent you one for a penny, thereby earning him the nickname "Scrooge." He saved the pennies and used them to buy flowers for the gardens he worked on at Sligo Junior High School in Silver Spring, Maryland. He used fluorescent colors, black lights—anything he could think of to make math fun and interesting.

Years after he retired and even after he died, I would still meet people who would say, "Amtower . . . did your father teacher math at Sligo?" Invariably, they would have stories about Pop, and how he helped them with something, made them get a concept in math, or perhaps simply helped them to pass.

In 1993, I was in a boardroom getting ready to participate in a discussion on marketing a huge government contract when this guy leans across the table towards me, and in a conspiratorial tone asked, "Did your father teach math at Sligo?" The guy was **Larry Rosenfeld**, president of Stackig Sanderson White, the largest ad agency in the government market, and we became friends that day, and we remain so today.

I am 56 as I write this (getting older, but far from done), and my father has been dead nearly 10 years, retired for 25 years, and it *still* happens. As a junior high school math teacher he made an impression so strong that he was remembered for decades. This is something worth emulating; to be so good, and so different at something, that people remember you fondly years later.

Though I work from home, and have for over two decades, I am almost always in the basement office by 7:30 A.M. and back in the office for an hour or four after dinner. I strive to be good at what I do, and being different just seems to come naturally.

What does all this have to do with my Laws of Survival and Success? And how do these laws apply in everyday life?

It's how I got here.

Law 10–The Law of Tithing

Tithing became important to me when I was coming to understand what it meant to be part of a group. As kids, we take turns doing the fun, or not fun, part of the game: being "it" in tag or hide-and-seek, pitching in baseball or softball. You had to give up the limelight, to share, so all could enjoy.

Of course not everyone wanted to share the limelight, sometimes those with better skills or the delusion that they had better skills. But these kids were outvoted in the games where we had all the kids in the neighborhood playing. Things were different when I was growing up in the 1950s and 1960s.

In every group you wish to be a part of, there are dues.

I remember the first time someone thanked me for being their mentor, and I was shocked. **Jay Weinberg** was a marketing manager at EDS in the early 1990s and we had several occasions to do things together. I do remember that he called occasionally asking for my opinion, but lots of people do that. Jay left EDS to take a job with Leo Burnett, a major Chicago ad agency, and he called to tell me of his decision and to thank me for being his mentor. I was floored. Jay went on to learn lots at the agency, then opened his own database marketing firm, The Jay Group, in Chicago, where he is doing very well. We are still in touch and try to get together whenever I am in Chicago.

In the mid 1990s, my friend Dendy was appointed CEO of GTSI, the company that bought his firm a year and a half earlier. I had done work on and off with GTSI and had many friends there, one of whom was the Marketing Director, **Lisa Dezzutti**. I called Lisa to say we could work together again, as I assumed Dendy would want me for some advice somewhere. Lisa told me of her decision to leave GTSI, not because of the management change, but because she felt the time was right to start her own business. I volunteered to advise her whenever she wanted—and often when she didn't. Her firm, Market Connections, is now 11 years old, and doing well.

Not long after Lisa started her firm, Dendy called to tell me another mutual friend was going to start his own business. **Richard Mackey** was also ready to go out on his own to do GSA Schedule (contract) consulting. So Dendy and I both helped Richard get started, offering what we could in the way of advice and client leads.

Mentoring is a great way to tithe, especially if you do so with no strings attached. So many people offered me advice along the way it is incumbent on me to return the favor.

Law 9–The Amtower Uncertainty Principle, or the Law of the Food Chain

Most of us use hyperbole on occasion. With some of us, the occasions just happen to be more frequent, or on a larger scale. And with some people, the childhood tendency to exaggerate does not go away.

People like this show up in all facets of our lives: as children, teenagers, and young adults in college, at work, at church, in the grocery store, or in the elevator. They are everywhere. And for the most part they are harmless. Take my **Uncle George,** for example.

George Arbogast was the husband of my father's mother's sister, my great Aunt Esther's husband. A Cumberland, Maryland native, he was a railroad man, having worked for B&O his entire life. Short and round, George was one of my favorite people growing up. Whenever we would go to Cumberland for the holidays, he always told stories that bordered on the bizarre, or what passed for the bizarre when I was a kid. His stories of his hunting prowess defied human skills, and I never doubted a word. He would also take me down to the train yards, introduce me to his friends, let me get in the cab of the big diesel engines, and let a kid be a kid, because part of him had never stopped being a kid. Everyone should have an Uncle George.

George was a very devoted and doting husband (he and Esther never had children), and he loved life. That *joie de vivre* was contagious. Regardless of the hyperbole in Uncle George's stories (even then, we suspected), he offered us hours of harmless amusement, which we not only gladly accepted, but the anticipation for an "Uncle George story" began when we got in the car to take the over three-hour trip to Western Maryland.

I believe there is a difference between those who tell exaggerated stories to children and those who bend the truth for personal gain. We've all heard the adage "cheaters never prosper," yet we see all too often that financially many do prosper, and not all get caught. What did this teach me?

I think we have all known people who have taken shortcuts that were not legitimate, and many of us have seen much worse. From my perspective, as limited and naïve as it may seem, these people are not complete, and they know it. They are a house of cards that can be blown over by a gust of fresh air. I have always assumed that these people live with the fear of being found out, and I believe living with that fear is just not worth it.

A minor epiphany occurred as I was writing this segment: There are many people who have been tangential to my life who will think this chapter is specifically about them. This reminds me of the Carly Simon song "You're So Vain"—you probably think this Law is about you. . . . I try not to keep negative influences in the front of my mind.

Law 8–The Law of Communication

When I was in college I worked at a telemarketing firm, renewing magazines over the phone. Yes, I was one of those people who called at dinner time. During the training before you got on the phone, **Chris Trelease**, the number two guy in the company (Sturner and Klein), taught us, among many things, the concept of the *word-per-idea ratio*. His desire was for us to use as few words as possible to get the sale, but I saw value beyond that, and kept the concept in the back of my mind. This was and is a great concept and a perfect phrase for conveying the concept of being concise. (I would like to point out that Sturner and Klein also taught us to be polite at all times and under all circumstances. It was an easy place to work and filled with great people.)

In undergraduate and graduate school, too many times I would catch myself stuck in a long explanation of something, and it became so long that I could not remember what I was explaining. "Not good, Kemosabe." (That's a 1950s joke. Kemosabe is what Tonto called the Lone Ranger. Tonto never used too many words.)

Law 7–The Law of Fidelity

It should go without saying that fidelity to your family is job number one, but I guess that still escapes some people. I really do not know what to say about that. So let me say something about a different kind of fidelity: unconditional friendship.

In the late 1990s, I spoke at the Vermont-New Hampshire Direct Marketing Annual conference. My friend **Scott Heller** had recommended me as a speaker, and the conference coordinators asked me to come. Scott was my first consulting client and we both learned lots through that relationship, which continues to this day.

At the conference, I met **Bill Heyman** (who attended my session) and **Amy Africa** (who was on the Board of the association). Bill gave me the most awesome testimonial—one I still use occasionally, and we became friends. Amy and I started a relationship that week that continues to this day. Amy evolved to become one of the most influential web site advisors. She speaks at many of my events; has been on my Board of Advisors since the inception; helps my clients when I ask; and we communicate frequently through email, rumor, and innuendo.

People are important to me because of who they are, not because of what they can do for me. If I can ever help them, it is always my pleasure to do so.

Law 6–The Law of Divine Right to Attention

We all want to believe that we are important in other spheres of influence. In the late 1980s I was advising a couple of groups pro bono, helping them with their government marketing programs. One of these was the National Computer Security Association. The principals at NCSA were **Bob Bales** (President and Executive Director) and **Paul Gates** (Marketing, COO).

In the mid-1990s when I was assembling my personal Board of Advisors, I was looking for my most successful friends to join and help me join those "most successful" ranks. I asked Bob, but he was very involved in a new project and said he did not think he could give me adequate time. He suggested Paul.

I expected Bob to say yes, and felt slighted when he said no. I shouldn't have. First, I had no right to his attention.

Second, he suggested to me an alternate that paid dividends beyond anything I could hope for. I called Paul and asked him to join the newly formed group, and he asked what I thought he could offer. I said something like we'll figure that out along the way!

The relationship that followed between Paul and me was nothing short of a continual and continuous epiphany. Paul is the embodiment of a hard-working man who mixes his Christian philosophy and his work ethic seamlessly. He does not proselytize by word, but by action. He offered advice in a few situations that were critical to me as I was coming to understand what religion really meant for me, and it became quite apparent to me that this man was a *moral compass*, and that our reconnecting was no simple accident of Bob Bales not having enough time. This was yet another road sign.

It is not about demanding or expecting attention. It is about earning some attention, and using it well while you have it. It is about respecting the time of those who give you the attention. They have other things to do, so do not abuse this privilege. It is about caring enough to reciprocate—and to offer them, and others, your attention, and to offer it not simply when it is convenient, but when it is needed.

Paul and I still call or email one another frequently on matters where we know we will get the attention we want: focused, one-on-one, from the heart.

Law 5–The Law of Spontaneous Generation

In late 1993, I called the editor of *Marketing Computers* magazine to give him some good-natured grief about removing my favorite parts of the magazine. I spent about an hour that day talking to **Dave Dix**, the editor. After my lighthearted jibes about removing the calendar of events (important to me as a marketer), he asked what I did and we ended up just talking for a long time.

When he was ready to get off the line, he asked if I minded if one of his editors contacted me the following week to do an interview. Wow. This was truly not my motivation when I called, but I did a three-hour interview with **Bronwyn Fryer** that came out in the March 2004 issue as a five-page interview and photo spread. All from one call, that had nothing to do with getting PR. They sent a photographer (and his assistant) to D.C. to shoot me on Capitol Hill for the article. The photo shoot took place the day after my daughter was born: November 6, 1993. Elora was born on Guy Fawkes Day. (My son Travis was born April 1 and my wife on May 5, Cinco de Mayo, once again confirming my suspicion that God leaves me cryptic messages everywhere. My birthday, September 1, is occasionally Labor Day, so occasionally I work.)

I had arrived! Or so I thought. I assumed after this brilliant piece of journalism by Bronwyn that clients and reporters would line up, fighting for my attention. This did not occur. I was largely inactive as opposed to proactive after this event; I thought the phone would ring. Indeed, a few of my friends called to say congratulations, but beyond that, nothing. No mad rush by the rest of the business press to follow up on this journalistic coup.

While my ego suffered a minor setback, I took inventory. How had the interview occurred? I called Dave to tell him he had removed a part of the magazine I found useful. I was giving him feedback. I had taken the initiative and got a wonderful unforeseen payoff. Then I did nothing. Hmmm. What if I contacted key people in the press regularly (when it was germane to their needs, or my perception of their needs), offered advice whenever I could, then did it again?

Since 1995, about a year after the *Marketing Computers* article came out and I had implemented my proactive "go to the press plan," I have appeared in well over 200 articles, often just a short quote. I am at the point where the press calls me more frequently than I call them. But I have never stopped calling them, doing as many favors as I can for my friends in the press. I also look for new reporters and new publications to target—anyone covering my beat of doing business with the government. I think it is safe to say that I am the most frequently quoted source on this topic in the country. But I work very hard at it, and I do not take it for granted. And there are some people out there who are envious of this exposure, but aside from whining, they seem to do very little to promote themselves.

How do I do this? Simple. Let me give you an example of a great press relationship I have with a guy who does not write about me. Every Monday **Richard Levey** of *Direct* magazine writes the "Loose Cannon" column for the Monday Direct e-newsletter. Richard is a funny guy and his columns generate many responses, among them on occasion are mine. We have developed a "pen pal" relationship via email, and occasionally on the phone, with the perpetual threat of getting together for a soda when we share closer proximity. My email "Letters to the Editor" often start with something like "Ricardo, the acid-tongued scribe," and his reply will come back "Amtower the Merciless." Ricardo is the kind of guy I would go out of my way for.

Law 4–The Law of Market Ownership

I get press and I love attention, but I do not own this market, the press, or really anything other than my reputation. No one "owns" this or any other market. I get press, and attention, because I work hard to make this market better. However, when the "good times" roll for someone or some company, hubris can—and often does—occur. I know it has for me, and I am embarrassed to say so.

I remember during the dot-com era when MicroStrategy was doing really well, one of their business development people approached me about one of my web-based projects. I told them a little about what I was doing, and they said not to bother—that they would be covering "all things web." The only thing MicroStrategy ended up covering with their drop from $300 plus per share to pocket change was lots of cement with their chalk outline. While the business development person is still in the market, I have yet to rub her nose in the statement. She has had at least two different jobs since then. Once upon a time I liked this person, but I am no longer certain about that. I guess I will have to make that judgment next time I see her, and measure any subsequent growth.

And my little web project? It turned into www.Government Express.com, which is doing quite well, thank you.

Let me say that besides my wife, there are two women in the market from whom I requested a favor. The favor is to pop my balloon if my ego gets too big. **Olga Grkavac** and **Anne Armstrong** keep me inside the boundaries of generally acceptable behavior, though I test the limits frequently. I did not ask any men to keep me in bounds for fear that they, like me, might not know where they are on most occasions.

Law 3—The Law of Creation

In the late 1980s I was the king of direct marketing to the government. I would tour Federal mailrooms with the mail managers, ask them what their problems were with mailers, and create venues to share these ideas with the vendor community, those trying to reach the government via snail mail (remember, this was pre-Internet).

For a variety of reasons there was a problem in several places within the government with getting mail inside the agency. Try as I might, I could do nothing to change this, at least not alone. It occurred to me that I might have more influence if I got the major trade publications behind a joint effort. The only problem here was the publications tended to feud and fight amongst themselves in a never-ending territorial battle for ad dollars. I knew all the right players and was determined to make a go of this, so I spoke to the person in charge at each publication, explaining carefully that only by doing this together could we benefit all.

In the late 1980s, the Association of Mailers to the Federal Government was born, and we conducted monthly meetings with mail managers from many of the major federal agencies, including the Department of Defense. The group was comprised of all of the trade publications, many from the contractor community, some ad agencies, and me. I chaired this group for almost two years until it merged with the Direct Marketing Association of Washington. We accomplished our goal of opening the agencies to some mail, especially the publications, and we demonstrated to the government mail management community that we were not simply "junk mailers."

During my time chairing this group I was asked by one senior member of the contractor community how I was making money from this. I indicated that I wasn't and there was no real way to do so, as this group was all volunteer, had no dues, and it was not why I started it. He looked like he did not believe me. So I said simply I saw something that had to be done, and I did something about it. Tithing and creation merge here, but you get the point. The guy asking me the question did not get it.

Law 2–The Law of Leverage

Several times over my career there have been those who have told others I am not very good at what I do. Others have said that they worked closely with me. Each was trying to leverage my name one way or another. Many times over the years I will have a friend call to tell me of someone trying to get into their good graces by either leveraging me as a resource, or by saying I did something my friend could not and would not believe. Rarely do I feel the need to confront anyone over these, as they have only damaged their own reputations.

At this point in my career, I have worked with hundreds of companies, and stay in touch with many I have worked with. I have also done thousands of favors expecting nothing in return. It is the least I can do because so many have done the same for me. I am comfortable in the space I occupy, and am willing to share it frequently with carefully selected company. But I am not willing to move, or be moved.

On the flip side of The Law of Leverage, I try to help people when I am in a position to do so. My friend **Mark Del Franco—Big D!**—from *Multi-Channel Merchant* magazine, was having a hard time getting through to a financial analyst I knew, a very well-respected guy. The analyst covered an industry Big D was writing about. Big D knew that I knew this guy, so he called and asked if I could help. I did a simple thing: I emailed my financial wizard friend and asked him to return the call to Mr. Del Franco. Within the hour, my analyst friend did just that, and I knew a little about how **Tom Hewitt** felt. Tom who? Keep reading . . .

Law 1–The Law of Gravitational Pull

Tom Hewitt was one of the most influential people in the government information technology contracting community from the mid-1980s through the late 1990s, when he sold his company, Federal Sources (FSI). Tom did lots of things right, but one of the many lessons I learned watching him was doing favors whenever possible.

He would do these many ways. When someone was between positions, Tom would print them up FSI business cards, give them some office space, and let them look employed. He would expect them to help FSI if possible, but the main thing was to make them feel needed during the interim period between jobs. And being at FSI would invariably help them find that next position.

Tom would also meet people in lobbies, when he was dining or having a drink, attending a reception, and he was always gracious with his time and knowledge. People would ask him about something, he would listen intently, and then recommend a couple of different courses of action.

I was on the Board of Advisors for FOSE, a major trade show in the government market, in the early 1990s. One morning **Christina Nelson**, the conference director, called me and she needed help. She could not get this General "X" at the Pentagon to return her calls, and she needed him or someone from his staff to speak during the conference portion of the trade show. She asked if I could help. I said "Sure," but had no idea who this guy was.

My first call was to Tom. His response was classic: "Oh, Buzz. Had dinner with him last Wednesday. What do you need him to do?" General "Buzz" called Christina within two hours, and I looked like a minor deity. A week later when I finally got around to thanking him, Tom had no recollection of the call. Just one more favor for a friend.

A few years later, I was talking with someone (someone who was renowned for his mercenary approach, the same unnamed someone who asked me how I was making money from the Association in Law 3) who was trying to tell me that Tom Hewitt was a low-life, nowhere near the man he pretended to be. I enjoyed telling this person that his opinion, in my estimation, was not worth anything to me from then on. This was not exactly how I told him, but I left no doubt in his mind that he was preaching to the wrong choir.

Tom Hewitt had gravitational pull, and with many of us he still does. From my perspective, Tom Hewitt knew instinctively that doing these kinds of favors, probably twenty times each day, would pay dividends. But it did not appear to be *why* he was doing it. He seemed to be doing it because he enjoyed it, he could, and because he would always feel better about himself for having done it, and because it helped the community in which he worked. I can never know that this was his real motivation, but he was always there for me when I asked (I was still a minor but rising player at the time), and I would return the favor whenever asked.

Casting bread on the water without expecting returns is one of the most important activities we can engage in. Doing favors that have caveats is akin to casting bread upon the water and attaching an anchor. Likelihood of return: zero.

CHAPTER 5

Why This Matters, and My Two Biggest Epiphanies

Why This Matters

I have a close friend I have known since the late 1960s. I met **Juli Maltagliati** when I started college, and we have been friends ever since, and through some bizarre times for each of us, the other has been there when needed, and remains so today. There is a warm feeling you get from friendships, from people who like you for you. This is very different from people who want to be close to you because it is advantageous. There is also a great feeling you get from knowing you are doing the right thing based on your own rules.

It really is that simple.

My Two Biggest Epiphanies

My two biggest epiphanies have nothing directly to do with my business but absolutely everything to do with my success.

Epiphany One

From the time I was 19 until I was 34, I developed and actively cultivated a drinking habit. I became proud of my bibulous propinquity, bragging about the amount of alcohol

I could ingest. In 1976, I bought a house with two friends I worked with who also imbibed. We worked in a restaurant, and beer was never in short supply, though we did have to stock up on harder liquor. Around 1980, I bought my partners out, but one remained as a housemate. The one who stayed was a former co-owner of the restaurant, and before that he was an aspiring manager in government, having attained a GS-14 rating (pretty high) in the Federal government at age 28. Shortly thereafter his wife came into an inheritance, and they purchased a tavern and turned it into a nice family restaurant. The husband began drinking regularly, and by the time I took a job at the restaurant, by all reports, he had changed. He was still a nice enough guy, but a very serious drinker.

Fast forward. I am living in the same house with this guy and the focal point of our lives was the drinking. Nothing happened without alcohol. Several tell-tale signs were posted for me: not knowing where I spent the previous evening; not knowing how or when I had returned home—if I made it home; not recalling apparently lucid discussions; and the like. I ignored and rationalized these as long as I could, until one night I took a long look at my housemate, remembered what he was in government, and a very bright light came on: *there, but for the grace of God, go I.* This guy was only eight years older than me (he was 42) and he looked like he was in his fifties, disheveled and always a little sloppy, a tremendously nice man, but on a severe downward spiral.

On December 10, 1984, I quit drinking alcohol.

Also on December 10, 1984, my first stray cat showed up. The last of my three dogs had died earlier that year, and the cats must have been waiting. I named the first one Henrietta, and I suspected she was a sign from God that my decision was a good one, but she was there to watch me, just in case.

At first I told myself that I was simply going to stop for three weeks to prove to myself that I was in control. After a week or so of sobriety, I was beginning to feel pretty darn good—waking up clear-headed, thinking about things other than "is there enough booze in the house for today?" which was an all-too-regular thought previously, and I was feeling good *about* myself.

Before Christmas, I told my then girlfriend, **Joanna Der-Stepanian**, and my parents that the three-week experience was now a life goal. I had made a deal with myself that I could not break—I gave myself my word. Joanna and Mom were ecstatic. Pop was pleased, but refused to think that I was an alcoholic.

I have not had a drink since whatever that last one was on December 9, 1984. And to be perfectly honest, I really do not remember that last drink. I think that is a pretty good start.

Three weeks after I quit drinking, on January 1, 1985, I started Amtower & Company.

Epiphany Two

In June of 2001, my friend **Jeanine Dorothy** and a friend of hers were at the movies. When they came out, it was dark, and the friend remarked that it would be nice to be able to go somewhere without all the suburban lights and look at the stars, as certain planets were aligning in an unusual pattern. Jeanine said, "We can go to Mark's house—he lives in the country and he has a telescope."

By this time I lived alone in the house the three of us had purchased in Ashton, Maryland—a three-bedroom rambler on three acres, two of the acres wooded. I also had four cats, all strays. I suspected that there was a sign that only cats could read in my backyard: "Silly biped inside. Will feed and love you. Just let him see you once."

The first three cats were girls, showing up between mid-1985 and late 1988. The fourth cat was a black male, and he showed up on my fortieth birthday during my birthday party—yet another sign from God that I was on the right track. It occurred to me if I stayed sober, I might end up with a couple hundred strays. I named the black cat Dude. Dude loved laps, and he drooled, a potentially embarrassing combination.

So they called, and they came, arriving after 9:00 P.M. I told them to bring dessert and I would make tea. Jeanine's friend was **Mary Ellen Podniesinski**, part of a group of folks who got together regularly to go to different ethnic restaurants. We had actually met a few months before at one of the dinners (a Korean restaurant on Route 1 in College Park, Maryland).

As soon as Jeanine introduced us I knew. I wasn't sure what I knew, but I knew. We were standing on the sidewalk behind my house. Before we started using the telescope, I gave Mary Ellen a guided tour of my backyard (which was quite large). It was dark and you could not see anything, and Jeanine was saying things like "You never gave me a tour of your backyard."

But now I knew exactly what it was I knew: This woman was a special woman, and once again I had a sign. They stayed for maybe 90 minutes. During that time I asked Mary Ellen at least five times if she would come to my party on the Fourth of July. Each time she reminded me that she would be elsewhere at a previous commitment. Maybe if I wait ten minutes and asked again. . . .

The next day I called Jeanine to ask for Mary Ellen's phone number. She hesitated, but I was very persistent (see the beginning of Chapter 1). I got the number. I called and asked her out. We went out to have dessert one evening. We started talking on the phone for hours at a time. I would go over and we would talk in her apartment.

Less than six weeks later I proposed, even though she did not attend the Fourth of July party. Okay, maybe sometimes I am one of God's quicker children. Proving the adage that the mouth can work independent of the brain, she accepted the proposal of a 40-year-old bachelor with a rat tail and a gold hoop earring, a guy that lived with four cats.

Worked for me!

CHAPTER 6

. . . And the Three First Laws

As my business evolved, and experience hit me over the head time and again, I knew something had to be done. So I came up with three rules to apply to all business situations. These three personal laws are on my company web site (www.FederalDirect.com) under the FAQs:

"Rumor has it you're hard to work with. Is this true? Probably. I am opinionated, and will express my opinions when asked—and sometimes without being asked. These opinions do not change when I move from audience to audience. I'm too simple for that, and I'm easily confused by distortions (my own or others). I have a simple business philosophy:

1) I don't do things I can't tell my wife and children;
2) I don't do things that are not fun (things I am not good at);
3) I don't take crap from things that breathe.

Violate any of these rules and I resign your account and refund your money. Life is too short.

Does this make me difficult? Possibly. Do I care? Occasionally, but not often. Life is too short to worry about things beyond your control, especially habitually rude people."

FYI: These rules were in place before I knew Mary Ellen. It started as (big surprise) I don't do things I couldn't tell my Mother.

I measure myself in two ways: what I think of myself, and what my wife and children think of me. These are simple measurements, and they are as valid as any I have seen. Will you take a moment out of your oh-so-busy schedule and hold a door for someone? Do you say "please" and "thank you" enough, and at all the right times, during the day?

After I started applying these three laws to each business situation, not only did my business life smooth out, but it began to grow more quickly.

CHAPTER 7
Final Thoughts . . . for Now

If you believe something is right, or wrong, you should say so. You may feel like "the voice of one crying out in the wilderness," but understand that wherever you are, there will be kindred souls somewhere close by, and your message will resonate. You are not a lone voice crying out in the wilderness.

I believe that *God lets no deed go unnoticed.* Good or bad, it does not matter.

Every now and again I tell Mary Ellen about something I did that day, something that made me feel good. Immediately thereafter I feel like I am bragging. Did I have to tell her? Wasn't the deed itself enough? I get over that quickly, because I often do not remember all the things I did between the time I left home and the time I return, and when I reflect at the end of the day, I can just smile and know. It can happen anywhere. In the office I will take calls and respond to emails, do favors, help someone with an issue, and move on.

Recently I gave a speech at a major budget conference, one started by Tom Hewitt 22 years ago. Before my talk I was seated in the audience between two guys, and I introduced myself. The guy to my right, **David Slenzak**, said, "You won't remember me, but when I was in graduate school I called you to ask some questions. You spent some time with me and aimed me at several helpful resources." I cannot put into words how this makes me feel. Casting this kind of bread upon the waters does come back in many ways, often in ways I can never know, but that's okay. It is not why I do it.

I do it because I can. The same reason that I still will give a couple dollars to homeless people on the street. I occasionally hear the mumblings of those who may be with me or near me (not Mary Ellen or our children), "You wouldn't catch me giving money to a bum for booze or cigarettes." I assume I am meant to hear and to feel rebuked for my foolish gesture. But I cannot assume these people are worthless bums who will squander the money I offer on alcohol or cigarettes. All I can think of is John Bradford in the Tower of London, seeing a prisoner on the way to be executed: "There, but for the grace of God, go I."

What I can assume is that God put these things in my path for the same reason he put my housemate in front of me in a certain light before I quit drinking, or the reason Henrietta showed up the day I quit drinking, or the reason Mary Ellen showed up when the planets were aligning, or the reason Stan Yablonksi called to tell me this conference he just returned from needed me to speak the next year, or any of the hundreds of epiphanies that presented themselves to me with no other explanation besides "Here is an opportunity for My child, who may not be the brightest or the quickest, but who might be able to do something with this because he won't let it go."

A life-changing event in one's personal life does not have to be huge in order to be significant, to have profound impact. Witness the one phone call with Joan April that led to adding *paid* consulting to my repertoire. The financial repercussions were enormous.

So, keep your eyes, ears, mind, and heart open, and the epiphanies will find you. Follow them and enjoy the journey they take you on. Do not let them escape unnoticed, un examined, and unused.

I'll see you at **www.EpiphanyBook.com**, where I hope you'll share your favorite epiphanies.

We are not through with each other, not by a long shot.

Vignettes and Comments from Those Referenced in This Book

I asked each of those mentioned in this book to provide their recollections to the event referenced. Well, I asked all those I could find. If you know where the others are, have them give me a shout via the www.EpiphanyBook.com web site.

I truly appreciate that they took the time to provide an epiphany somewhere in our past, and that they took the time to write about it now. In other instances where I was asked to help, or offer advice, I was flattered that others thought me capable of providing guidance, especially early on, like when Jay said thanks for being my mentor. It is difficult to express how much this kind of trust and respect means to me, and I have tried to never take these relationships lightly.

That these people *bothered* to tell me something, ask me something, offer me an idea or venue, or otherwise share, showed me they cared. These were not things they had to do, but things they chose to do. These are the actions that truly define who we are: the act of offering an epiphany, and the act of doing something with it. They bothered to go out of their way for me, and to each I owe a debt of gratitude.

There are many, many more, but this is a short book. These are all good people, and I am happy they are part of my life.

Here they are, unvarnished and unedited, in the order they arrived, sort of a litmus test on how I am doing so far. I publish these not to feed my ego, but to demonstrate that one person can make a difference. And I am trying not to get cocky, Lynn, but I have always had a hard time with humble.

Judy Bradt, www.SummitInsight.com

The only time Mark's advice has been ineffective is when I didn't follow it.

When I met Mark, his business was three years old, and I'm pretty sure that Lynn Bateman introduced us. In 1988, I had just arrived at the Canadian Embassy knowing nothing about how the U.S. government bought (or, really, DID) anything. My job was to help Canadian companies—especially ones in information technology—win government contracts. I had a lot to learn, and fast. Mark was selling mailing lists—inexpensive, clean lists—of government technology buyers. I needed guests to invite to receptions, and, eventually, to Canadian company presentations that I hosted. His lists were perfect . . . and his advice was easily the most forthright that I could offer to my clientele. I knew that his insights—straight from the head and the heart—would immediately appeal to everyone who heard him speak. His recollection of an "aw-shucks" dust-kicking speech just goes to show you that he needed to see himself in a different light.

Our relationship grew quickly beyond that. Mark—being a generous human being with a giving mentality—decided he wanted to befriend me from the very beginning.

He always had time to answer my questions—which were many then (and still are today). I was on the lookout for wise people with hard-to-find insights to share. When I started hosting groups of visiting companies to Washington tech trade shows, I wanted them to hear from the smartest straight-talkers I knew. I am deeply allergic to slick fast-talkers and puffball speakers offering marketing schlock, and wanted to protect my clients from people who would confuse them and take their money. Mark taught me his epiphany lessons by walking his talk. He stood out then, and still does today, because he speaks his mind, stands up for people of integrity, and is candid about (and steers clear of) those who offer poor value or obviously don't see eye to eye with him on his Ten Laws. And he gives and gives. And the Universe notices.

His integrity and steadfast honesty—including being willing to admit and learn from his mistakes as well as share those lessons—makes him a beacon in a town where even its most prominent leaders, time and again, think that those values are not worth time and attention . . . and, time and again, are proven wrong.

When, after 15 years, I left the Canadian Embassy and launched my own consultancy, Mark immediately offered his heart and brain and time in support. Since 2003, he has been a willing sounding board for my ideas, and continued to offer me the unvarnished truths about developing a consulting business. I am grateful beyond measure for that . . . exactly because there are still dozens of people all too eager to take my money and promise me things I don't need or results they can't deliver.

Even beyond advice I call and ask for, Mark is a man of determination, vision, and integrity. He knows why he walks the earth . . . and to watch him walk his path is instructive for those of us who feel we're still finding our way.

Don Libey, www.Libey.com

Mark is an enigma. The first time I met him at the Chuck Tannen reception for speakers, I pegged him for an enigma. He was clearly different, and totally natural. Here was a person who called it like it was, said it like it is, and uncompromisingly stood by his principles and beliefs. He is a "genuine article," "one of a kind," unique and good.

Over the years, we met now and then and exchanged ideas. His were common sense, logical, and came from a motivation of decency and betterment. When I left one of these visits and drove home, Mark's character and integrity accompanied me and caused me to rethink many of my own ideas. They still do, all these years later.

Perhaps my encouragement to write a book has some part in the writing of this many-faceted jewel, I don't know. I do know that his humanist accomplishments, his peers' respect, and his professional integrity perfectly balance his enigmatic uniqueness. And he has been responsible for a lot of companies having a lot of success in business-to-government marketing. I am eternally proud that he considers me a friend.

Amy Africa, www.EightByEight.com

This is a book chock-full of laws by the biggest outlaw I know.

I met Mark Amtower in the early 90s at the VT/NH Direct Market Group's Annual conference. He had been introduced to our organization as "the guru of government marketing." At our first meeting, I learned two things about Mark. One, he's not the guru, he is THE only guy who knows literally anything AND everything about Fortune I (government) marketing. Two, when Mark speaks on TV, radio, or anywhere else, you need to evoke a 7-second delay; his vocabulary, like his speech, is nothing if not passionate.

I've always thought Mark would be the guy who threw himself an early funeral to see exactly what people had to say about him. This chapter of the book is it. The thing is, that unlike most people, Mark doesn't do it for the ego boost (his is already slightly larger than Texas), he does it to see how he can improve himself. With the cast of characters he surrounds himself with, he knows that even if he picks up just one kernel it will have been worth it as his quest for excellence is truly like no other.

In my professional life, I've been blessed with more than anyone should ever hope for. There are three people who have really influenced my career and made it, and me, the Internet marketer I am today. Mark Amtower is unequivocally one of them. Over the years, he's not only been my "go-to guy" for government and other general direct marketing advice, but for personal advice as well. He's been my friend, my confidante, and more than I care to admit, my kick in the ass.

His advice is always blunt and to the point, for example: never take crap from anything that breathes and never do anything you wouldn't tell your mother about. He's honest, fair, and has a sense of humor that is drier than the Sahara. Unlike most consultants, Mark is not an actor. He never pretends he knows something when he doesn't. Nor does he tell you things you want to hear, just because you pay him.

He tells you like it is and then, if applicable, he helps you improve it. Mark once told me that if you define yourself by what you say and what you do, you'll never leave yourself to be misinterpreted or repositioned by others. This book, and its immutable laws, are just that, Mark Amtower at his finest.

Maggie Bedrosian, www.MaggieBedrosian.com

"Amtower calling" is a welcome topic designator on my incoming email. I haven't seen Mark in person in about four years since I relocated to the Seattle area. But such is his continuing hold on my respect that my cursor moves promptly to open the message. "What's he up to now?" I wonder.

I open the email and once again bask immediately in the Amtower presence. (I almost said "aura," but that word feels too fancy for this rustic, irreverent sage from Cumberland.)

I think we first met at the Tower Club in Virginia. I was amazed at his earthy, opinionated style. *"How does he survive,"* I asked myself, *"in the business environment where a polished patina often outshines real content?"* He was intrigued to learn of my book on public speaking. We soon got into a great discussion about my theory on the importance of "the message from your marrow, the authentic things that are true all the way to the center of your bones." He experimented eagerly with several ideas I offered, learning from both his successes and misfires.

All these years later I reflect that he has always "gotten away with" his "unique" style for seven reasons:

- He honestly knows what he is talking about.
- He tells the truth.
- He wastes zero energy on BS or pieties.

- You'll never catch him spouting anything merely popular or convenient (unless it's also entertaining!).
- He uses elements like surprise, irreverence, and laughter to help listeners unlock their thinking, opening themselves to new possibilities or original ideas.
- He applauds talent, wisdom, experience, and accomplishment in others.
- He nurtures long-lasting loyalties.

I guess all this reflecting makes me wish we all demonstrated these qualities to the degree that Mark does.

What I do know is that whenever "Amtower (is) calling," I'll be listening.

Joan April

Mark Amtower was too nice. He gave away much too much valuable information. In some cases he was charging too little. In some cases he was charging nothing. Is this any way to run a business? NO! I had to tell him to actually charge money for what he knew. He isn't in the poor house so obviously it was good advice. Until recently, I hadn't spoken to Mark for many years. He paid me back. He gave me business advice and still didn't charge me anything. . . .

Michael Brown, www.MichaelABrown.net

Because epiphany is such a big word, some people think it has to be noisy . . . like a sudden thunderclap that jars us awake at 3 A.M.

Certainly, an epiphany can be powerful, but it can be gentle, too. I believe an epiphany can occur when a person quietly opens his or her mind to the knowledge and insights that have lived within them for a long time. The "epiphany" emerges when the embedded "ah-has" gain a language with which to express themselves.

Mark and I have spoken many times about marketing to government and to business. Our dialogue has helped confirm that success in both those realms demands discipline, not a series of tricks . . . the long view, not a campaign or medium of the moment . . . a reverence for and attention to humanity, not callousness for a quick buck.

No noise, no thunder, and it's not 3 A.M. . . . but what an epiphany!

Lynn Bateman

As a columnist for Government Computer News (GCN) in the 70s and 80s, being a Federal "action" analyst was a necessary avocation. Digesting contents of the Federal Register each day; gleaning facts and opportunities, was a necessary backdrop for my articles on government acquisition and management. One learns that if ill-prepared or under-informed, successful Federal marketing is unattainable. From the start, Amtower was a sponge absorbing what became raw material for his own corporate credibility.

After several years of research, reading, and writing, seminars were a natural complement rounding out my own full-service Federal contracts counseling firm. Mark's aptitude told me that he could build his own business. Hard work and intellectual curiosity were his recognizable winning attributes.

Literally thousands of eager sales and marketing reps became our students and, quite often, our clients. Once in a while an individual would distinguish him/herself by winning profitable and productive contracts. Mark not only observed, but applied his observations to pragmatic business. If I was a "mentor" for Mark, it was in helping him distinguish classy, knowledgeable winners from puffing, phony losers.

Unlike sales in other markets, successful Federal sales requires a deeper dimension in the person selling. Depth of character in Washington, D.C. was no more common in those days than it is now.

So along comes Mark Amtower. Our initial acquaintance was occasioned by us working for the same publication, but Mark was exceptional as a budding entrepreneur. Perhaps my experience with so many students and clients had sharpened my insight, but I discerned that Mark possessed all the elements of a successful Federal guru.

Initially concentrating on building mailing lists, Mark wasn't just printing labels. He was crawling inside mailrooms to meet and apprehend secrets of productive Federal direct marketing. Amtower's ability was obvious in seminars I taught for our publisher—Mark's lists and brochures packed every class. Between 20 and 40 students paid several hundred $$ to attend and no one left without getting more than their $$'s worth. Amtower knew how to turn testimonials into business development. It was a pleasure to invite Mark to address my classes from time to time. He needed to build his Federal "rolodex" and sharing my contacts with Mark was never risky. Amtower can be trusted.

Seems Mark's acumen went far beyond lists and brochures. His intellectual depth drew him into my classes, but his self-confidence needed a boost. Giving Mark cues and tips was never a waste of my time. "Amtower calling" meant that Mark had taken my words to heart, pondered their application for his own life, and was calling to verify that he "got it."

Amtower always "got it" and then some. Now Mark "gives it." And "it" is his winning way.

Irv Greenberg, ATD American

I've never known Mark Amtower to suffer fools gladly, so when he began his lunchtime speech at the 2005 MeritDirect Co-op, I knew it would be something special. And Amtower's Laws of Survival and Success sure didn't disappoint.

Well-known for his expertise on Government Marketing Best Practices, Mark delivered what amounted to a treatise on Best Practices for Business and, more importantly, Life.

It deeply resounded with most who heard it and I'm glad he's expanded it into this book.

Based on a 15-year relationship with my company as his client, I can say Mark is true to his philosophy. His code of business conduct and actions bespeak integrity and loyalty.

In an era of double-talking issue-straddlers, Mark is succinct with a refreshing candor. Yes, he's opinionated, but with the facts to support his position.

He's an expert who's unafraid to say "I don't know," and who will, without hesitation, refer you to others for the answers.

He's a fine teacher and communicator, whether sharing his knowledge one-on-one or in off-white papers on his website.

His seminars are extremely well-organized and packed with valuable and current information. Unlike many speakers who guard their data and have you scribbling madly in the dark, Mark's seminar workbooks include all of the slides being presented along with plenty of room for notes.

Mark works hard at his craft; he *cares* . . . and it shows.

Mark has always espoused to know your niche and what motivates your niche.

Well, when his niche is mentioned, the Law of Gravitational Pull will certainly apply—the name of Mark Amtower will come up quickly and first.

Mark Del Franco, *MultiChannel Merchant*

Mark Amtower is one of the few people I've come across who says what he's going to do. Period. The influence this man wields in and out of Washington is remarkable. Sources who were reticent to speak with me suddenly seemed eager participants after getting a call from Amtower. I've run across far too many consultants who talk just for the sake of talking. Not Amtower.

What's more, it's not only the sources he keeps but the veracity of the information contained on an Amtower phone call. More often that not, when Amtower calls, I know he's got the goods. And as a reporter, you can't ask for more than that. When he says it's going to rain, better take an umbrella.

Dendy Young

The memorable people in life, I find, are those who have passion and show it. Mark is the epitome of passion. Everything he does, he does with passion. He writes and speaks with passion; he teaches dummies like me the fundamentals of marketing with passion; he connects people and advises them with passion. Above all, he cares about people with passion. Not just his immediate family—Mary Ellen and his daughter and son—but everybody, or, at least, it seems like everybody! Mark has a huge and generous heart.

I think the factor that has earned Mark the respect that he has in the community is that people know that Mark always tells the truth. Bold, caring, always unvarnished, truth. And Mark is very perceptive—his model of the universe includes the nuances. There have been times when I have not liked the truth—such as the times when my company has run a stupid ad campaign or executed poorly in a trade show. But I always read his analysis and, strangely, when he was talking about some other company, always agreed with him. When you listen to Mark, you learn.

As I was reading this book I became conscious of how well Mark knows himself. Being able to clearly articulate the heuristics by which one lives one's life is no mean feat. It forced me to think: do I live by the same standards? Could I write my standards down? Where and how would they differ? It is clearly beneficial to be able to articulate them. . . .

This book unabashedly exposes the inner Mark. At the end of it, you like and respect him more than you did at the beginning.

Scott Heller, www.NationalAVSupply.com

As Mark's first consulting client, I have the dubious distinction of working with him in his most unvarnished state. Surprisingly, the ensuing years have done very little to alter his style—or his patina. This is a good thing, because any added polish would have the deleterious effect of watering down his "Amtower-ness," both in content and in impact!

For nearly 20 years Mark has provided me with a frequent and consistent barrage of unique business recommendations, straight talk, and provocative life advice, much of which can also be applied to one's personal life to reset and re-tune our moral compass. In a world where too often paid consultants are toadies who tell you what they think you want to hear, Mark's straight talk is a refreshing and welcome slap in the face.

I am grateful to Mark for the many insights that have helped us grow our business, but more importantly for the ensuing personal friendship and support that has developed between our families over the years. Thank you Mark, you've done your parents proud.

Those who know him refer to Mark's inspiring nuggets of truth as "Amtower-isms." He is truly a unit-and-a-half who speaks his mind without fear of retribution. Please keep it coming!

Stan Yablonski, Data-Pages, Inc.

Data-Pages was started in 1983, pre-PC days, when we were selling 8" diskettes, disk packs, and $18 gender changers to corporate America. Around 1985–86 I was fortunate to attend a seminar entitled "How to Sell to the Federal Government" hosted by a Mark Amtower. Immediately I was taken by his knowledge and passion for the government marketplace. Mark had rounded up some industry insiders and the whole event was very crucial to the direction we started to migrate to. I sat at one of his evening roundtables and was convinced we had missed, in the federal government, a major market.

The following year I attended a Direct Marketing seminar and trade show for catalogers. It was good, but I came away with the knowledge this event was missing something valuable . . . Mark and his government insight.

Upon returning to New Jersey, I called Mark (no email around yet) and said "You need to be there and they need you." I encouraged him to contact the organizer's name I had and, fortunately, for all parties concerned, he did.

Leap forward to 2007 and Data-Pages does 99 percent of their IT sales to the federal government and prime contractors. We've survived 24 years partly because we followed Mark's knowledge and implemented it effectively. As I contemplate retirement and the future sale of my "baby," all the best wishes to Mark. As everyone who knows him knows, he has his own style, and his tombstone will probably say "I did it my way." He's a true icon in the industry.

Lisa Dezzutti, www.MarketConnectionsInc.com

I met Mark Amtower in the late 1980s when I started my career at GTSI. He had the best federal mailing lists in town and was unmatched in his knowledge of federal marketing. Whenever a new vice president came on board, I always had Mark in for a reality check session. I still refer him today to clients entering the government market for that dose of reality—and even to those that have been around for a while, but need to be reminded of the Law of Divine Right to Attention.

Mark lives by the rules in this book. I have never met anyone, outside of my grandnanna, who gives as selflessly as Mark does. He is always volunteering ideas and looks for ways to help others succeed without seeking anything in return. Mark is what I call "good people"—down to earth, honest, ethical, and smart with a lot of heart. Unfortunately people like Mark are too often few and far between in this life, particularly in business.

Mark has always been a phone call or email away when I've needed a sounding board. This has been especially true over the last 11 years as Market Connections as grown. I have not followed all of his advice—yes, from time to time I too suffer from the couch potato syndrome! But I always welcome his advice and often seek it out. He is a valued colleague and more importantly, a treasured friend.

Jay Weinberg, www.TheJayGroup.com

Mark Amtower is clearly one of the most influential people in my career.

While I have had a number of mentors throughout the years, I've never asked anyone to play that role. I don't even seek out mentors. When I meet people I admire, I just seem to start asking questions and explaining the business issues I'm having. Some people actually take the time to help. After a while, I realize that I have a mentor.

When I met Mark, I saw first-hand the real qualities of a successful entrepreneur. He found a niche, and had the ability, the drive, and the confidence to make his dream come true. I found myself asking questions, and Mark was always happy to answer and give advice.

By watching Mark work and talk about his business, I was excited about starting my own. When I finally did, telling Mark about it was one of my proudest moments.

To this day, I have fond memories of him talking about his "tricks of the trade." While he may have been discussing marketing to the government, what I heard was the value of finding a specific niche and becoming the best there is.

Mark focuses and never strays. And that's the main ingredient of a champion.

More than 12 years out of D.C., I am still proud to consider Mark a mentor, and always look forward to the e-mail subject line, "Amtower Calling."

Bill Heyman, www.SupremeAudio.com

Refreshingly honest! For some that's an advertising slogan. For Mark, it's a way of life. Loyalty and honesty are the cornerstones of his being. He IS refreshingly honest and fiercely loyal to his family, his friends, his clients, and to his country! He's also loyal to himself . . . which makes it imperative for him to say what's on his mind . . . often to the astonishment, enlightenment, and delight of his audience!

Even on a great day, Mark lacks the "bamboozle" factor! He never tries telling you something just to let YOU know that HE knows it! He tells it like it "is" . . . and if you are on the wrong side of "is," his presentation might be the longest, most uncomfortable day of your life. On the other hand, if you can recognize what needs to change in your company based on his observations, it might be the most profitable day of your life.

During his presentation you certainly will recognize a number of things that you have been doing right forever. You'll also probably recognize a number of things you do which land on the "other" side of the ledger. However, just one or two new tidbits of information from Mark can make the difference between a successful and expanded Business-2-Government marketing campaign or a continuation of the rut-based strategy you're currently using.

Following some key suggestions made by Mark, we have become a successful Open Market vendor and have built a very loyal following in the Federal market, especially the Department of Defense. Those buyers recognize the core values (which we share with Mark) of honesty, loyalty, quality merchandise, and service. For us it's a way of life . . . not a strategic plan.

Sheila J. Schaetzke, K+K America

While it's true that I met Mark at the Direct Marketing to Business Conference in 1994 and, over the years, Mark has provided an incredible (and I mean incredible!) amount of insight and knowledge with regard to the Federal Government market to the National Business Furniture (and now, K+K America) companies, I think very highly of Mark for many other reasons. I'm not sure when we first realized we have a United Methodist Church background connection; we do. I'm not sure when we first realized we have wonderful and beautiful children fairly close to the same ages; we do. I'm not sure when we first discovered we both like theatre, specifically musical theatre; we do. The Mark Amtower I know is so much more than the foremost expert on marketing to the Federal Government; he is an incredible human being—husband, father, friend, and professional.

JoAnna Brandi, www.CustomerCareCoach.com

You're right Mark, God does leave cryptic messages everywhere.

I met Mark by reputation long before I met him in person at a Merit Direct Co-op Meeting many years ago. I knew "of him" before he started his company, while he was still working for Gary Slaughter. At that time I was part of the B-T-B mailing list community, which was small. Reputation said it all, and he had a good one.

Long after I moved from that business to my own, Amy Africa got us talking and encouraged our friendship. I think she thought the combo of his big, tough, wry personality and my "touchy feely" customer caring slightly woo-woo one would be amusing. It turned out to be both that and *amazing*.

I've known Mark so long, he still had color in his wardrobe. Amy happily introduced us in person after Mark had just done a presentation. "Good job," I commented, "Never knew there was so much to know about government marketing. What's that?" I pointed to an insignia on his green shirt.

Mark had the word "Doubt" embroidered inside a red circle with a slash on his shirt.

"No doubt." Mark said.

"No doubt about *what*?" I asked.

"Just NO doubt," he said.

"What does that mean, no doubt? Everybody has doubt, you have to have doubt, if you don't have doubt you can't be open, you *have to have* doubt."

"Nope. NO doubt."

And so in earnest began a friendship with a man that has more faith in me than I had in myself at times. Mark is rock solid, and constructs his life one brick at a time, lovingly, knowing that brick is part of the strong foundation of a very large cathedral.

Epiphanies, indeed.

Juli Maltagliati

It's hard to know where to begin to describe Mark Am-tower. In a weird antithetical way, he is both an easy-to-read open book and an impossible-to-define enigma. I've known him since 1969-long enough ago to seem like another life-time ago, and in many ways, it was. We were friends from the very start. In recent years, I have also worked for Amtower & Company as an independent contractor, and feel very fortunate for the opportunity—in all my job experience, I've never worked for a more fair or more generous employer.

But I know him best as a friend. Mark is a man who has created and recreated himself, shaping his life to his pref-erences at any given time, and doing it with what has seemed an enviable ease and aplomb. Though struggles are in-evitable in any fully lived life, Mark's distaste for whining or focusing on the negative has made his struggles seem far less strenuous than they no doubt were.

I witnessed Mark evolve from heavy drinker to con-firmed teetotaler, from semi-impoverished anarchist to successful entrepreneur, from longtime bachelor to de-voted husband and father. His evolution has been more like revolution, really, so radical have been the shifts—and all have been self-chosen, self-defined, and self-created. Yet throughout the wide spectrum of roles filled and lifestyles engaged, at his deepest core—in the ways that count the most—Mark has remained very much the same.

There are traits that have been steadfast in Mark throughout the decades: his enduring honesty and in-tegrity, and his uniquely twisted sense of humor. Anyone who encounters him, however briefly, isn't likely to miss them. It would be hard to walk away from time spent with

Mark not feeling uplifted in some way. At least, in almost 40 years, I never have.

Vic Hunter, www.HunterBusiness.com

Mark has written his "Epiphanies" with the heart of his mother and the mind of a wise leader—not just a business leader, but a life marker. Mark walks his talk with Law 8: The Law of Communication.

I find that the ability to look at ourselves objectively and share that vision with authenticity is rare. Yet, Mark's stories lead us to the simplicity on the other side of our complex days. Mark has taken his lifetime to mine those truths from Mom's life as golden nuggets, not polished and somewhat raw yet of great value. The 10 Laws are more like Commandments than a list you might find on Letterman.

Over the years, I have picked up my relationship with Mark, enjoyed it, and laid it down for some time. Yet, whenever I picked up the relationship, Mark has been passionate, alive driven to make a difference and to bring value to those he touched.

I like Mark Amtower. I have liked Mark for two decades every time our journeys have crossed. Mark says he is not God's quickest child, but I can see he is His child.

Richard H Levey, Senior Writer, *Direct magazine*

Maggie Bedrosian very neatly summed up my thoughts when she mentioned Mark's earthy, opinionated style. I was tempted to copy her words wholesale and submit them under my own name. What stayed my pen was that (a) I don't live in Seattle, and (b) the Tower Club in Virginia hasn't let me in since the noodle incident, which for the sake of decorum I will not recount here. Because of these two facts, her words would not ring true coming from me.

Instead, let me say this: There is nothing spontaneous about the law of spontaneous generation. To paraphrase Ian Fleming, one erudite letter from a knowledgeable source is a happenstance. Two erudite letters from a knowledgeable source is a coincidence. Three erudite letters from a knowledgeable source is the product of equal parts sweat and intellect.

There isn't a writer in the world, with the possible exception of J. D. Salinger, who doesn't appreciate thoughtful reaction to his or her work. Here's an ironclad rule: By dint of having read something, you are qualified to comment on it.

Mark, you've already internalized this: I mention it for your readers.

What's second-best about Mark's communications is that he never asks for anything except that his points be considered. I have a special place in my heart for people who dash off a one-sentence comment about my latest column, followed in the same communication by a two-page pitch for whatever they're selling. This special place is bilious and acidic.

What's best about Mark's communications is that they are often curmudgeonly, always respectful and reliably informed. Even when we disagree, it's clear his comments are written with respect—and that's how they're read on this end. (They're also a hell of a lot of fun to receive.)

As for the benefits that may or may not accrue from taking the time to write: Readers, having your letters printed reinforces your name in whatever industry you happen to play in. But more than that, in Mark's a constant stream of considered responses has built his brand (with me, at any rate) as a valuable source, should I ever need insight into marketing to government.

We may or may not cross soda straws someday, but I will always look forward to crossing swords.

Tom Hewitt, Founder, Federal Sources

Mark and I started our companies at about the same time. Our businesses were focused on the government market with similar target clients, but we were not competitors. We had similar challenges and a lot to learn. Mark quickly became a trusted business associate, adviser, and good friend. It was a time when I desperately needed a friend and someone who I could trust, someone who would tell me if my ideas were OK or just plain stupid.

As our separate businesses grew and as we survived the start-up phase, we had new challenges. The conversation moved from how the government procurement system worked to what changes we should expect. Our clients expected more strategic advice along with the day-to-day tactical guidance. At a breakfast we would analyze why some smart people failed and some other average people succeeded. We analyzed the rollercoaster trends in federal procurement and winning business plans. We enjoyed critiquing their marketing programs. We also noted the companies and people who were trustworthy that we wanted as clients and those to avoid.

Mark has made great contribution to our federal business community. I believe he loves this business the way Patton loved a war. He is passionate about being well-informed and having a vision for how the market will change and what to expect. He is fun to work with and his professional integrity makes him a trusted partner.

As I move toward retirement, I have little interest in starting another business. However, if I did start a new business, Mark will be my first call to get a sanity check. I feel fortunate to have met Mark early in my business career. It's been exciting. I continue to read and listen to his advice, his "off-center observations," and his epiphanies. Life is good and friends make it better.

Thanks for the many years of guidance.

Joanna Der-Stepanian

Mark has been an outstanding friend for more than 25 years now. I can testify that he does truly live by his words, and walks his talk. He is not afraid to step outside the stream of popular thought and opinion; rather he operates out of his own value system, and does what he thinks is right. Yet, he is open and willing to hear and consider new ideas or ways to look at the world. He will hear an opposing viewpoint, think it over, and sometime later it will be obvious that he gave it due consideration and thought and is willing to revise his own stance to incorporate the new information.

He is indeed constant in the ways that count. Witness his decision to stop drinking, just a little deal that he made with himself in 1984, and 23 years later he has stuck with it. His loyalty as a friend is unmatched. This extends to the numerous ex-girlfriends still in his life, who he has converted to lifelong friends.

It is now amusing to think that my initial impression of him was to find him somewhat intimidating! In reality he is all heart. If it were not enclosed in his chest, his heart would take at least three days to walk around. When I think back on the many ways he has influenced me since first meeting him in 1981, his philosophy of "no regrets" looms large. It has been such an incredible pleasure to see him able to transition these life strategies into a successful and respected business, and to see that he did not have to compromise them or leave them behind in order to succeed!

Anne Armstrong, President and Group Publisher, 1105 Government Information Group

The appealing thing about Mark Amtower is that no one else has the same view of the world as he does. It's always different, sometimes dramatically different.

You also never have to wonder what Mark's agenda is. It's right out front.

You never have to wonder what he thinks about something or if he is going to tell you straight out.

I don't always agree with Mark, but I am always interested in what he is thinking. His 10 laws of survival are an excellent guide to managing business and life.

Larry Rosenfeld, www.AboutSage.com
Mark and Me

Mark Amtower and I both grew up in Montgomery County, Maryland. We were native sons, the same age, living parallel lives with similar life experiences as we grew up during the conservative Cold War 1950s. As we left our teens, we enjoyed the freedom of the 1960s that came with hippie era. And then we settled down (somewhat), entered business, and started families (some later than others). Coincidently, we ended up in complementary businesses, serving the marketing needs of government IT companies.

Even though it seems like just last week, the first time I actually met Mark was about 20 years ago. We were in a meeting at the old PRC building. He introduced himself to me. When he mentioned his name, it sparked a memory. I leaned forward, stared into his eyes as I usually do when I get intensely interested in a conversation, and asked him, "Did your father teach math at Sligo Junior High School?" The answer was a quick "yes," and he asked me if he was my teacher. I said yes, and that he was a great teacher—strict and tough but fair. That was the beginning of a long acquaintance that has since turned into an endearing friendship.

Our paths have crossed too many times to count over the last 20 years. I attended some of Mark's seminars, saw him at government IT meetings and events, read his newsletters, and listened to him on the radio. I always have and still do enjoy his biting sarcasm and *"tell it like it is"* commentary. I admire his ability to see through the bull, and reply with a cutting remark that is right on target.

Since I founded Sage Communications three years ago, Mark and I have seen and talked to each other much more frequently. Our conversations regarding mutual business interests and issues surrounding the community led to the founding of the Government Marketing Forum. Based on the first event, The Forum is sure to become the Number One venue for the industry.

As we get older and wiser, I visualize the two of us sitting at the Tower Club reminiscing about the good old days that we are now living as part of the most exciting business in the world.

Book Two—"There Are No Couch Potatoes on This Bus"

Coming Soon to a bookstore near you!

Visit
www.EpipanyBook.com
for continuing details!